# Contents

# What's in a name?

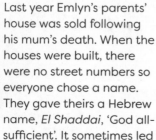

Last year Emlyn's parents' house was sold following his mum's death. When the houses were built, there were no street numbers so everyone chose a name. They gave theirs a Hebrew name, *El Shaddai*, 'God all-sufficient'. It sometimes led to interesting conversations, not least with Dr Graham, their Jewish GP!

Two writers in this issue mention the names of God. Phil Winn leads us into Exodus, where God reveals his name to Moses. He is Yahweh, the unchangeable I AM. New writer Toby Hole (he wrote a Spotlight on the parables in a recent issue) leads us through three key chapters of John's Gospel which testify to the truth in Jesus. Again a name is central: Jesus says, 'I am the bread of life' (6:35).

New writers are not the only recent changes in *Daily Bread* – we are now following a new syllabus. Each series lasts for just one or two weeks. Over the next four years, we will read the whole of the New Testament and something from every book of the Old Testament.

Another change is that the Spotlight series has a new theme. Each time, one of our contributors will write about their own experience of the Bible – when they started reading it, how God has spoken to them through it and so on.

Ro Willoughby starts us off with her very personal story of how the Bible helped her to become secure in her faith when she was young, and has sustained her through life since.

So let's remember that '*El Shaddai*' – 'the God who is more than enough' – is with us!

**'Tricia and Emlyn Williams**
Editors

# Daily Bread toolbox

:ia & Emlyn
iams
ked with
pture Union
many years.
yn led Schools
istry, then
ked with SU
rnational.
ia was also
t of the
ools team and
r worked for
Publishing,
eloping and
ing Bible
urces. In
ent years,
ia has been
earching
d writing
ut faith
d dementia.
v living in
folk, they both
tinue their
ing, editing
d talking-
h-people
istries, and
involved in
cal Anglican
rch.

### WAY IN

This page introduces both the notes and the writer. It sets the scene and tells you what you need to know to get into each series.

### A DAY'S NOTE

The notes for each day include five key elements: *Prepare, Read* (the Bible passage for the day), *Explore, Respond* and *Bible in a year*. These are intended to provide a helpful way of meeting God in his Word.

### PREPARE

Prepare yourself to meet with God and pray that the Holy Spirit will help you to understand and respond to what you read.

### READ

Read the Bible passage, taking time to absorb and simply enjoy it. A verse or two from the Bible text is usually included on each page, but it's important to read the whole passage.

### EXPLORE

Explore the meaning of the passage, listening for what God may be saying to you. Before you read the comment, ask yourself: what is the main point of this passage? What is God showing me about himself or about my life? Is there a promise or a command, a warning or example to take special notice of?

### RESPOND

Respond to what God has shown you in the passage in worship and pray for yourself and others. Decide how to share your discoveries with others.

### BIBLE IN A YEAR

If your aim is to know God and his Word more deeply, why not follow this plan and read the whole Bible in one year?

# Patience pays off

Despite serious health issues in his retirement years, Roger Purdom has become a Faith Guide and continues to introduce young people to Jesus. He shares some of his story, and talks about the importance of building relationships and why we all have a vital role to play in building the church of today and tomorrow.

Roger has had a long association with Scripture Union; he went on his first SU camp in Arthog near Barmouth in 1964. Later he became an SU team leader, helping on different holidays until 1981.

For many years, he was a teacher at a school in Croydon, and ran SU holiday clubs at the church where he was an elder.

Then he moved to East Sussex to take up the headship of a Christian boarding school. He began his final job in 1995 as pastor of an independent church in Littlehampton. Roger recalls, 'We launched summer holiday clubs at church, using SU resources, and I did those until I retired. Each year we had 60 to 70 children attending.'

## The break that got Roger into schools

When Roger first moved to Littlehampton, he wanted to do Christian assemblies in schools, but initially there was quite a bit of resistance. The break came when one school heard that he was trained as an OFSTED inspector. 'In those days, spirituality was one of the aspects that OFSTED inspected. The school asked if I'd come and do Christian assemblies to help them pass their forthcoming inspection.

'Word got around; soon I was going into ten primary schools. Those doors have never closed, not even during COVID! Instead they asked me to do assemblies on Zoom. That suited me too because by then I'd developed some quite serious health issues.' Even so, Roger has managed to do over 100 assemblies in the past 2 years.

'The kids know I'm going to tell them a Bible story and pray, but I usually get a positive reaction and a listening ear from them.

'I hope to get back into schools eventually, but for now the doors are still open and I'm still doing Zoom.'

## Sharing his testimony

'One head at a C of E school asked if I could do some sessions on the Trinity and prayer. Afterwards, he said, "The kids loved it, so now can you do some sessions on characters in the Bible whose faith was tested but God brought them through?" So, I did Ruth, Esther, Mary, Peter and others.

'Then he asked, "Can you talk about how your faith has been tested and how God has brought you through?" I did three sessions: one on when I was a teenager and first came to faith, one during my teaching years and one on my church pastor years.

'These talks were also publicised in emails to parents, and when my wife went into a local shop an assistant said, "Oh the kids love Roger and his assemblies!"'

## Camp always oversubscribed!

In 2003, Roger started a summer camp for local children. 'We took them to the beach – it was a first for many of them, even though they lived so close by,' Roger recalls. 'We played games; they got soaking wet and filthy dirty and had an incredible time!

'Eventually we had to move. We relocated about 10 miles inland to Lodge Hill, an activity centre. During the day, the kids would do all sorts of adventurous stuff which they loved – abseiling, mountain biking, climbing. In the morning and evening we'd have Bible stories, worship and a talk.

'Out of the 60 children already booked onto this year's camp, about 90 per cent won't have heard a Bible story other than one we might have shared at an assembly. Parents know it's Christian, but every year we are oversubscribed.'

### The domino effect

Roger recognises the enormous value of building relationships. 'If you want to draw children into a relationship with God, you have to first build a relationship with them. And by connecting with them in different situations – school, camp, church – you get to know not just the kids but the parents and teachers too.

'It's vital to build genuine friendships across the community, seeking to serve that community. It's not just about what *you* want – what will *they* value? One time the churches in Littlehampton did a meal for head teachers at the end of each academic year to thank them for what they do with the children and young people in our area, and for allowing us to partner them on that journey.

'While we serve, we are so often blessed. One church in our Littlehampton group was in a village called Lyminster. When its new curate started a family service, it had a great response and attracted families from much further afield because they knew us from camps and assemblies. It's like a domino effect: all those different contact points are interlinked.'

### The value of church volunteers

It takes time and patience to build those genuine community-wide relationships. 'That's why I feel ordinary church members of all ages have a vital part to play,' Roger says. 'If the relationship only resides with the church leader or youth worker, it can falter if those people move on, which they often do. Not all church leaders have the skills or experience to work with young people either.'

Becoming a Faith Guide through SU really helps those church volunteers who are taking that role, as Roger has found. 'It recognises that this is a long-term process, and provides training, encouragement and access to resources.' There is also the opportunity to network with and learn from other Faith Guides.

Roger plans to keep sharing the good news of Jesus with children and young people for as long as God enables him to do so. 'We mustn't give up on the next generation. What kids are being exposed to via their phones, computers and TV is frightening. And the world is changing so fast that we can't keep up with the trends.

'More than ever, young people need to hear that God is there for them, that he loves them and will never, ever change – he's the same today and for ever.'

Please pray for Roger and all Faith Guides as they commit their time and skills to helping children and young people to learn more about God. If you would like to know more about becoming a Faith Guide, visit su.org.uk/faithguides.

A shorter version of this story first appeared in *Connecting You*, Scripture Union's free quarterly supporter magazine. If you'd like to receive copies of *Connecting You* and learn more of how God is moving in the hearts and lives of children and young people today, you can sign up on our website at su.org.uk/connectingyou.

# The true and the new

John's account of the hours leading up to Jesus' death and the days immediately following his resurrection takes up nearly half his Gospel. The chapters preceding these show us, through his teaching and prayers (John 13–17), the priorities that Jesus longed to leave with his followers. Concluding that time, Jesus starts his journey towards the cross and – looking over John's shoulder – we join him.

In narrating events, John's writing is rich with recurring themes, meaningful contrasts, stark irony and eyewitness details. His stated purpose (20:31) is to engender life-giving belief in the truth of who Jesus is. These chapters alone highlight Jesus as the true Shepherd, true High Priest, true Passover Lamb, true Son of the Father, true King, true Adam, and Truth Himself. Another theme to look out for, especially in the second half of our series, is the newness that opens out of the empty tomb: new life, new faith, new peace, new purpose, new perspective, new calling, new wholeness – to name but a few! What truth about who he is might Jesus want to reveal to you this Easter? What newness might he be waiting to lead you into?

As we come to contemplate the Passion, let me invite you to ask God for the grace to be present to Jesus in his suffering, to 'sorrow with Christ in sorrow' (Loyola), allowing that to deepen your walk with and love for him.

### About the writer
**Cath Butler**

Cath enjoys working as a peripatetic music tutor, and she has just qualified as a spiritual director. Her primary 'love languages' are the clarinet, pancakes, walks by the sea, reading and journaling. She writes for and edits @PilgrimsPages – a social media hub designed to help people explore journaling as a spiritual practice.

# Starting over

## PREPARE

Reflect on the lyric, 'All things once sown in weakness you raise in promise'.* What do these words stir in you?

## READ

John 20:11–18

## EXPLORE

Left at the tomb, Mary is still walking grief's valley, her path darkened by the disappearance of Jesus' body. Resurrection is not on her radar. Through a haze of tears, the appearance of angels seems not to unsettle her – all we hear is her desperation: 'Where is he? Where have you put him?' How she longed to assuage her loss by completing his body's hasty burial (Mark 16:1). So, in this garden, Mary 'mistakes' the second Adam for a gardener (another Genesis reference: Adam was created and commissioned to tend the earth).** I wonder how often we encounter Jesus without realising, distracted by our despair or determination...

What cuts through the confusion is a voice, a name (v 16). At creation the Spirit brought shape to the chaos and God's voice formed light and relationship from the void. Now Jesus speaks a new era into existence – restored and renewed relationship between mankind and his Maker (v 17) – beginning with the person in front of him. He doesn't start with emperors or aristocrats; he doesn't even start with the twelve... He starts with a woman, insignificant in her society. Our God is not afraid to start small, and he invites us into the same (Zechariah 4:10).

'Do not hold on to me ... Go instead to my brothers and tell them, "I am ascending to my Father and your Father, to my God and your God."'
John 20:17

## RESPOND

List some of the ways God has started small in your life. Thank him and ask for his help to see other small beginnings in and around you.

*Sam Yoder, 'All Things Rise', Mercy/Vineyard Publishing, © 2015
**Tom Wright, *John For Everyone: Part 2 Chapters 11–21*, SPCK, 2002, p146

**Bible in a year:** Joshua 1–3; Psalm 37

**Tuesday 2 April**
John 20:19–23

# New peace, new purpose

## PREPARE
Pray: 'Lord God, let me receive the peace and purpose you have for me today.'

## READ
**John 20:19–23**

## EXPLORE
A lot can happen in a day! One that began with burial rites, a missing body, angels and accusations now brings us to these locked doors, and leaderless disciples (v 19). One that saw a tomb of breathless confusion turn to belief, and a garden of grief turn to gladness, now shows us a room of fear. Having suspected graverobbers themselves, were the disciples afraid that the Jews would claim they had stolen Jesus' body (Matthew 27:64)? Yet all our anxious, agitated defences are no barrier for Jesus. So we watch as fear fades in the powerful presence of peace.

And that peace has a purpose. Every person of the Trinity participates in passing Jesus' mission on to his disciples. The perfect 'Sent One' (as John often refers to Jesus) has completed the work entrusted to him by the Father and invites his disciples to continue it, equipped by the Holy Spirit. Sent 'as'

Jesus was (vs 21,22), how are we to walk in our purpose? Whether others receive it through the gospel we preach or from us personally, forgiveness is primary (v 23). So, on this first day of the week, as at creation, chaos is brought under control by the Word of God as the breath of God is given to his people again.

> Again Jesus said, 'Peace be with you! As the Father has sent me, I am sending you.'
> **John 20:21**

## RESPOND
Which rooms in your life have you locked because of fear? Ask Jesus to pour out his peace, to show you his purposes and to breathe on you again.

**Bible in a year:** Joshua 4,5; Romans 10

# Seeing through scars

## PREPARE
**Look at and touch a visible scar on your body. What story does it tell? (If you can't do this, perhaps you could ask someone else.)**

## READ
**John 20:24–31**

## EXPLORE
Poor Thomas. Despite the 'doubting' badge he has worn for centuries, this clarity-loving disciple was all in (11:16) and these verses are no exception. Last of the remaining twelve to meet the risen Jesus, Thomas is first to call him 'my Lord and my God' (v 28). This is what all of John's carefully chosen words, his whole skilfully woven account, have been leading up to (v 31). Beyond the bounds of doubt this Jesus is truly God, and within the welcome of new belief he offers us new life.

So how does Jesus usher Thomas into his new faith? We might notice the close parallels between Thomas' stubborn declaration and Jesus' later suggestion (vs 25,27). Or perhaps what strikes us is the quality of evidence Jesus offers – his scarred yet living and present body was surely proof of both his identity and his resurrection. But what draws my attention is that Jesus invites Thomas into his wounds, into the story of suffering and sacrifice they tell, and into the hope of his pain made whole. What strength and safety there is in knowing that the one asking for our trust has borne brokenness for us. Stepping into his wounded heart we see things differently, touched by the truth of who he is and how he loves.

> ... he said to Thomas, 'Put your finger here; see my hands. Reach out your hand and put it into my side. Stop doubting and believe.'

**John 20:27**

## RESPOND
Imagine Jesus welcoming you into his wounded heart, a place there set apart for you. Journal about what this experience stirs in you.

**Bible in a year:** Joshua 6,7; Romans 11

# Anyone for breakfast?

## PREPARE

Reflect on what Jesus has called you to – your hopes, experiences, the challenges, the celebrations.

. . . . . . . . . . . . . . . . . . . . . . . . . . . . . . . . . . . . . . . . . . . . . . . . . . . . . . . . . . . . . . . . . . . . . . . . . . . . . . . . . . . . . . . . . .

## READ

**John 21:1–14**

## EXPLORE

With the Passover festival over, the disciples are back in Galilee. Back home, back to all that had been familiar before the seismic shifts their world has undergone since they left. Was that why Peter wanted to get back to work, to get back to normal (v 3), to fill his hands and help him process all that filled his head and heart? Or was going fishing his best attempt at moving into his new mission? Whatever his motives, the scene that unfolded must have resonated clearly in Peter's memory. Not so long ago, after another long and futile night on the same lake, Peter had obediently let down his nets on the other side of the boat and been overwhelmed by the catch (Luke 5:1–11). That was his first commissioning from Jesus.

When something similar happens at this stage, what is John trying to tell us? Yes, it is a symbolic recommissioning. Yes, it is a reminder to listen for Jesus' voice and obey his words – no matter how counter-intuitive they seem. Yes, it is a promise of unimaginable – but not unbearable – fruitfulness as we work with him. But it is also an invitation to breakfast. Jesus loves partnering with us, receiving if not relying on our efforts (vs 9,10). But what he wants most is our presence.

> Jesus said to them, 'Come and have breakfast.' None of the disciples dared ask him, 'Who are you?' They knew it was the Lord.

**John 21:12**

## RESPOND

What might it look like for you to accept Jesus' invitation to breakfast – to bring yourself and your efforts and allow him to nourish you?

. . . . . . . . . . . . . . . . . . . . . . . . . . . . . . . . . . . . . . . . . . . . . . . . . . . . . . . . . . . . . . . . . . . . . . . . . . . . . . . . . . . . . . . . . .

**Bible in a year:** Joshua 8,9; Romans 12

# Going back to go on

**PREPARE**

Spend a few minutes simply resting in the loving gaze of the One who knows you best.

**READ**

John 21:15–19

**XPLORE**

I remember, as a child, wincing while my mum held firmly to the hand that had a splinter lodged in palm or finger. It astonished me that something I'd barely noticed entering could be so excruciating to remove. But if it stayed in, the risk of inflammation and serious infection was real. We tend to associate splinters with our physical bodies, but our minds, hearts and memories can receive them too – words that echo in our ears, scenes that flash before our eyes, stabs of recollection that haunt us and hold us back. Those things – things we can't unsee, unhear, unsay or undo – live on within, causing inflammation, infection, even immobility.

That's why in this passage, with three probing questions (vs 15–17), Jesus takes Peter back to the night of his denials. Jesus is gentle and firm in his pursuit. Peter protests (v 17). If God knows everything, even what's going on inside

us, why does he still ask us to express it when doing so can be painful? The answer we see here is that he has more for us. Through Jesus' three questions and his own pained responses, Peter receives the reinstatement and release of renewed trust, as well as the reminder that all he does flows from love.

> The third time he said to him, 'Simon son of John, do you love me?'
>
> John 21:17

**RESPOND**

Pray: 'Lord God, thank you that despite my failures and mistakes you continue to trust me and use me. May I live fully and freely from your love today.'

**Bible in a year:** Joshua 10,11;  Psalm 38

# Living for legacy

## PREPARE
Draw a map of the path your life has taken so far.

. . . . . . . . . . . . . . . . . . . . . . . . . . . . . . . . . . . . . . . . . . . . . . .

## READ
**John 21:20-25**

## EXPLORE
John's final scene may have been included to disperse the rumour he references (v 23). To tell that story, he had to set it up with the rest of the chapter – and we are the richer for it. Imagine the gap that would be left if we knew nothing of that awe-filled breakfast on the beach, or Jesus' intimate walk with Peter! What if Peter had preferred John's lot and spent his time writing a fifth Gospel rather than laying the foundations of the early church? However small or strange our story may seem, living into God's plans for us leaves a mark. Yet when it gets hard, how easy it is to hesitate. Like Peter (vs 20,21) we look around, wondering what others are up to, whether we'll face this future alone or if there might be an alternative.

Jesus' response refocuses us on all that matters: 'Follow me' (vs 19,22). The paths he has for each of us start and end in different places, traverse different terrain and last for different lengths. In places they cross, or run alongside each other, but no two are the same. Any anxiety that stirs is settled when we remember that he is both ahead of and alongside us (Deuteronomy 31:8), writing new chapters of his story in, and with, our lives (v 25).

> Jesus answered, 'If I want him to remain alive until I return, what is that to you? You must follow me.'
>
> **John 21:22**

## RESPOND
Reflect on Ephesians 2:10. Ask God to show you, this week, how his words in your flesh continue the story of his Word made flesh.

. . . . . . . . . . . . . . . . . . . . . . . . . . . . . . . . . . . . . . . . . . . . . . .

**Bible in a year:** Joshua 12–15;  Romans 13

# Humble, held, hopeful

**PREPARE**
Talk to God about your memories and experiences of silence, positive and negative.

**READ**
Psalm 131

**EXPLORE**
One of the soul-refreshing joys of living in Northern Ireland is being able to walk in the Mourne Mountains. There, with the crunch of my footsteps stilled as I pause to enjoy the views, I have often remembered Elijah's experience of God in the sound of sheer silence (1 Kings 19:12). External silence is hard to come by in today's fast-paced world, internal silence perhaps even more so among the strong currents of our frenetic thoughts and fraught feelings. Yet that is what this psalm invites us into with beautiful brevity: a calm and quiet soul.

Three themes interweave: being humble (v 1), being held (v 2) and being hopeful (v 3), each leading into the next. Do you notice from verse 2 that we have a part to play: we calm and quiet ourselves? As we reject arrogant, controlling attitudes that preoccupy us with what's not ours to oversee, we discover a contented peace. No longer reliant on small feeds of milk, a weaned child is sustained for longer periods by more substantial solid foods and has learned over time to trust the reliability of the one who feeds them, attaching securely in the process. What if we could experience this confident, steadying attachment with God? Surely, our hope for both present and future would be firm and enduring.

> But I have calmed and quietened myself, I am like a weaned child with its mother; like a weaned child I am content.
>
> **Psalm 131:2**

**RESPOND**
Why not try including a time of silence in your daily rhythms with God? Start with just a couple of minutes and gradually increase.

**Bible in a year:** Joshua 16–19; Romans 14

# Jump into a **new** adventure this summer!

## Can we count you in?

**Volunteering with Scripture Union is more than just an adventure, it's life-changing!**

Each year we host action-packed, faith-filled holidays and missions for hundreds of children, helping them create lasting memories while having the time of their lives! Could you take a break from the day job and volunteer with us?

**FIND OUT MORE AND REGISTER TO VOLUNTEER:** SU.ORG.UK/COUNTMEIN

Scripture Union

# The name of the Lord

Later this month, Jewish families will celebrate the feast of Passover, retelling the suffering of the Israelite slaves in Egypt and their dramatic rescue by God. The story of the Exodus is quoted in the psalms and the prophets (eg Psalm 78:12; Jeremiah 2:6) and is central to the identity of the people of Israel.

We do not have an exact date for the Exodus. Some have suggested the pharaoh in question may have been Rameses II, but the Bible does not name him. The central character of the book is not Pharaoh, or even Moses, but the Lord, the God of Israel. Through successive plagues (in chapters 7–11) he reveals himself to Pharaoh until, finally, he is forced to submit to the Lord's authority.

At the beginning of the book, the children of Israel, having been in Egypt for several generations, seem to have become less familiar with their God. In this book the Lord makes himself known, revealing his name to Moses, to the Israelites and then, through dramatic displays of power, to Pharaoh and the Egyptian people.

God's name revealed to Moses shows him as Yahweh, the unchangeable 'I AM' (Exodus 3:14), upon whom his people can depend. It was a name so holy that later Jews dare not pronounce it, but it was the foundation of their faith.

As the psalmist later said: 'Some trust in chariots and some in horses, but we trust in the name of the LORD our God' (Psalm 20:7).

About the writer
**Phil Winn**

Phil is now retired from full-time ministry but occasionally leads worship and preaches. He and his wife Pauline enjoy exploring the local countryside and spending time with their grandchildren.

## Monday 8 April
### Exodus 1:1–22

# Holy disobedience

## PREPARE

Reflect on situations where it might be appropriate to follow the apostle Peter's dictum: 'We must obey God rather than human beings!' (Acts 5:29).

## READ

**Exodus 1:1–22**

## EXPLORE

In Jerusalem's Yad Vashem holocaust memorial museum an avenue of trees commemorates people who resisted Nazi pressure to rescue Jews from the holocaust. One of them is dedicated to Oskar Schindler, hero of *Schindler's List*, the German industrialist who saved many Jews from the gas chambers.* Today we read of others who defied the commands of a despot to secure the safety of the children of Israel.

At the end of the book of Genesis, a grateful pharaoh welcomed Joseph's extended family, the children of Israel (Genesis 47:1–12). As the years pass, the descendants of these economic migrants increase in number. When a new pharaoh (probably from a new dynasty) assumes the throne (v 8), he views the immigrant community not as a blessing but as a potential threat. Does this portrayal of an immigrant community sound familiar?

To keep the Israelite community under control, Pharaoh first enslaves them (v 11), then tries to stem its growth by killing newborn boys (v 22). Two midwives defy Pharaoh and let the boys live. When questioned, they say that Israelite women have especially short labour. When is it acceptable to be less than truthful to the authorities? Much to the frustration of historians, the name of this pharaoh is not recorded, but Shiphrah and Puah, the disobedient midwives, are remembered by name.

The midwives, however, feared God and did not do what the king of Egypt had told them to do; they let the boys live.

**Exodus 1:17**

## RESPOND

Against which injustices should you act? Pray for persecuted minorities.

*www.yadvashem.org/righteous/stories/schindler.html

**Bible in a year:** Joshua 20–22; Psalm 39

# Israel cries out

## PREPARE

'The righteous cry out, and the LORD hears them; he delivers them from all their troubles' (Psalm 34:17). Tell God about your current situation.

## READ

Exodus 2:1–25

## EXPLORE

Yesterday we met Shiphrah and Puah, the midwives who refused to put to death newborn Israelite boys. Today we meet Moses who survived birth because of them and who lives on because of the extraordinary actions of his mother and sister, quietly defying the orders of Pharaoh.

Despite his upbringing in the Egyptian court, Moses is aware of his Israelite origins and grows into something of a tough guy, killing an Egyptian taskmaster (v 12) and later rescuing Reuel's daughters from some bullies (v 17). Yet neither the quiet defiance of the midwives nor Moses' impulsive action can make a decisive difference to the plight of the community of Israelite slaves.

The slavery lasts until (and beyond) the death of this pharaoh, causing the Israelites to cry out (v 23). Then something happens. The Lord – so far hardly mentioned in the book of Exodus – hears their cry. His concern will lead to action: 'It is the cry that begins the narrative of rescue and salvation.'* Sometimes it may seem as though God has forgotten us and needs to be reminded of our plight, but could it be that he is waiting for us to cry out for help?

> God heard their groaning and he remembered his covenant with Abraham, with Isaac and with Jacob.
> Exodus 2:24

## RESPOND

'The LORD is close to the broken-hearted and saves those who are crushed in spirit' (Psalm 34:18). Pray for a situation you know about where individuals involved feel crushed and hopeless.

*W Brueggemann, *Delivered out of Empire: Pivotal Moments in the Book of Exodus Part 1*, John Knox Press, 2021, p5

**Bible in a year:** Joshua 23,24; Romans 15

# What's in a name?

## PREPARE

**Spend a moment to prepare to enter the presence of the Holy One.**

## READ

**Exodus 3:1–22**

## EXPLORE

I knew a minister who said that he always made sure he was well-dressed and wearing his shoes before he went into his study to pray, because he could not come before the Lord in his carpet slippers. Moses removes his shoes as a sign of reverence when he is on holy ground in God's presence. Might we sometimes be too casual in our approach to God?

Does it seem strange that Moses asks God what he should say if the Israelites ask for the name of the God who has sent him (v 13)? Over 2,000 gods were worshipped in Ancient Egypt,* each with their own area of responsibility. Perhaps the people have become unfamiliar with the God of their ancestors, Abraham, Isaac and Jacob (v 15).

'I AM who I AM' is, in Hebrew, linked to God's name Yahweh (usually written YHWH and rarely in use today). What does this say about the nature of God? The name Yahweh is so holy that Jews would not pronounce it, sometimes substituting the word 'Adonai' (Lord) and sometimes using the consonants from the divine name with the vowels from Adonai, pronounced 'Jehovah'. Most English Bibles translate it as 'Lord'. Can you think of a time when you learned something new about the person of God?

> God said to Moses, 'I AM who I AM. This is what you are to say to the Israelites: "I AM has sent me to you."'
>
> **Exodus 3:14**

## RESPOND

Pray: 'Jehovah, great I AM! by earth and heaven confessed; I bow and bless the sacred name forever blest.'**

*World History Encyclopedia*, www.worldhistory.org/article/885/egyptian-gods-the-complete-list/
**D ben Judah, 'The God of Abraham Praise', trans T Olivers, 1770

**Bible in a year:** Judges 1,2; Romans 16

# Reluctant hero

## PREPARE
What are your strengths and weaknesses? Ask God to equip you for his service.

## READ
**Exodus 4:1–17**

## EXPLORE
Moses faces huge challenges. He will have to confront Pharaoh and demand the release of all the Hebrew slaves, but first he must meet the Israelite elders and convince them that the God of their ancestors can rescue them (3:16–20). God *will* rescue his people, but they need to have faith. Notice how many times the word 'believe' occurs in these verses. Our salvation is wrought by God; our response is to believe. Sometimes we need to trust God to do the seemingly impossible.

Moses trusted in the Lord who appeared in the burning bush and who promised to be with him (3:12). Now God gives him three miraculous signs with which to convince others. When Moses is still reluctant, God reassures him that he will provide the words he needs (vs 10–12). But he still asks to be excused from this mission (v 13).

God is not pleased, but agrees to send Aaron as a spokesman for Moses, as Moses is a spokesman for the Lord. What does this say about the way in which God works with us? Does the Almighty modify his strategies to accommodate our responses? Would the later story have been different if Aaron had *not* been Moses' right-hand man (eg see Exodus 32)?

> But Moses said, 'Pardon your servant, Lord. Please send someone else.'
>
> **Exodus 4:13**

## RESPOND
Is God calling you to take on a new challenge or responsibility? Talk to him about your feelings. Pray for those you know who are sharing God's good news today.

**Bible in a year:** Judges 3,4; Proverbs 1,2

# Hard heart, hard questions

## PREPARE

**Meditate on these words: 'Blessed is the one who always trembles before God, but whoever hardens their heart falls into trouble' (Proverbs 28:14).**

## READ

**Exodus 4:18–31**

## EXPLORE

Some Bible passages present challenges to the interpreter. This has at least two! First, after all the Lord has done to prepare Moses for a confrontation with Pharaoh, he says that he is going to make it more difficult by 'hardening Pharaoh's heart' so that he will not agree to Moses' demands (v 21). At other times Pharaoh hardens his own heart (7:13; 8:15).

We will see that, as successive plagues come, Pharaoh becomes more and more stubborn, until the death of Egypt's firstborn causes him to relent and allow God's 'firstborn' to escape (12:29–32). Our attempts to find simple solutions to the problem of God's sovereignty and human free will are doomed to oversimplification. We can only hold the two in tension: God is sovereign *and* he respects our choices.

What are we to make of the revelation that the Lord, who has chosen and prepared Moses for this great task, is 'about to kill him' (v 24)? Gershom, Moses' firstborn son, has not been circumcised as required of Jewish males (vs 24–26; see Genesis 17:14). The situation is rectified and the ritual performed. It's a reminder that the leaders of God's people need to observe the same rules as the rest of God's people to maintain fellowship.

The LORD said to Moses, '… see that you perform before Pharaoh all the wonders I have given you the power to do. But I will harden his heart so that he will not let the people go.'

**Exodus 4:21**

## RESPOND

Ask God to show you if there are any areas where he wants to challenge you, but you are resisting his will.

# Gotta serve somebody

## PREPARE

'Help us to know you that we may truly love you, so to love you that we may fully serve you, whose service is perfect freedom' (Augustine).

. . . . . . . . . . . . . . . . . . . . . . . . . . . . . . . . . . . . . . . . . . . . . . . . . . . . . . . . . . . . . . . . . . . .

## READ

Exodus 5:1–21

## EXPLORE

Moses and Aaron gain access to Pharaoh's court and, once there, make an audacious demand (v 1). The Hebrew verb 'used' demands more action than simply *letting* people go. John Goldingay suggests: '*Send* my people Israel off so they may hold a festival for me in the wilderness.'*

Why should Pharaoh acquiesce to this (v 4)? He does not even know this God of the Hebrews. Over the next few chapters of Exodus we will see the Lord revealing himself to Pharaoh, who gradually, grudgingly, learns to acknowledge that the Lord is King.

The Israelites will eventually be freed from their slavery in Egypt to hold a festival to the Lord in the wilderness (12:31). Their leaving will be marked with the feast of Passover, and they will travel to Sinai – probably Horeb where Moses had met with God at the burning bush (3:1–15) – and the place where the covenant between the Lord and his people will be established (Exodus 19,20). Freedom from slavery meant freedom to serve the Lord. As Paul wrote: 'Now that you have been set free from sin and have become slaves of God…' (Romans 6:22). As Bob Dylan sang: 'You gotta serve somebody, it may be the devil or it may be the Lord, but you gotta serve somebody'.**

> Pharaoh said, 'Who is the LORD, that I should obey him and let Israel go? I do not know the LORD I will not let Israel go.'
>
> **Exodus 5:2**

## RESPOND

Pray for someone you know who, like Pharaoh, does not know the Lord.

*J Goldingay, *Exodus and Leviticus for Everyone*, John Knox Press, 2010
**B Dylan, 'Slow Train Coming', Columbia Records, 1979

. . . . . . . . . . . . . . . . . . . . . . . . . . . . . . . . . . . . . . . . . . . . . . . . . . . . . . . . . . . . . . . . . . . .

**Bible in a year:** Judges 7,8; Proverbs 3,4

# Where God touches the earth

## PREPARE

Meditate on these words of Paul: 'I pray that out of his glorious riches he may strengthen you with power through his Spirit in your inner being, so that Christ may dwell in your hearts through faith' (Ephesians 3:16,17).

## READ

**Psalm 132**

## EXPLORE

2 Samuel 6 and 7 give the context for this psalm. King David occupies a palace in his new capital, Jerusalem, but the Ark of the Lord is in a temporary tent, as it had been in the tabernacle throughout the wilderness wanderings. He brings it in procession into the city but is not allowed to build a permanent home for it. That task would be completed by his son Solomon.

This psalm was traditionally sung by pilgrims to Jerusalem to celebrate festivals. As they ascended the hill they remembered David's wish to see the Lord at home in Jerusalem. Mount Zion (v 13) is one of the hills on which Jerusalem is built and came to be used as a synonym for the city.

David could not rest until he found a way for the Ark, the visible symbol of God's presence, to be at home in his city. We have an even greater privilege; by his Spirit he lives in each one of his children.

There is no longer a splendid temple in Jerusalem, where people can go to meet with God, but Christ has made a way for us to enter the presence of God in the heavenly tabernacle (Hebrews 10:19–22). Let us not neglect the opportunity to meet with him.

'Let us go to his dwelling-place, let us worship at his footstool...'

**Psalm 132:7**

## RESPOND

Is the Lord welcome in every area of your life?

# Let battle commence

**PREPARE**
Ask the Lord to give you a fuller understanding of his nature.

. . . . . . . . . . . . . . . . . . . . . . . . . . . . . . . . . . . . . . . . . . . . . . . . . . . . . . . .

**READ**
**Exodus 5:22 – 6:12**

**EXPLORE**
When Moses complains to the Lord that his visit to Pharaoh has only made things worse, the Lord promises that he will change Pharaoh's mind.

First, the Lord reminds Moses of what he has told him before: he is Yahweh, the great 'I AM'. He is the same God who has revealed himself to the patriarchs, Abraham, Isaac and Jacob. Although the name 'Yahweh' does occur in Genesis (eg Genesis 4:6), God revealed himself to Abraham and the patriarchs primarily as God Almighty (*El Shaddai*; eg Genesis 17:1). Now he is seen as the great 'I AM' who is with his people. As *El Shaddai* the Lord made a covenant with the patriarchs and promised them a homeland. He has heard the cry of the captives, will rescue them and will take them to the land he promised their forefathers.

Moses may have been reassured by this, but fearing even worse treatment from the Egyptians, the Israelites are unimpressed when he tells them of God's promise (v 9). Moses seems to be back at square one (v 12). Have you ever had your confidence knocked when you tried to tell others something you believed God was saying to you, but they did not share your enthusiasm?

'I appeared to Abraham, to Isaac and to Jacob as God Almighty, but by my name the LORD I did not make myself known to them.'
**Exodus 6:3**

**RESPOND**
Pray for any individuals or churches who are feeling despondent because of the obstacles they face or because their efforts seem to go unrecognised.

. . . . . . . . . . . . . . . . . . . . . . . . . . . . . . . . . . . . . . . . . . . . . . . . . . . . . . . .

**Bible in a year:** Judges 11,12; Psalms 42,43

Exodus 6:28 – 7:13

# Snakes alive

## PREPARE

**Tell the Lord about challenges facing you today.**

........................................................................

## READ

**Exodus 6:28 – 7:13**

## EXPLORE

Moses is still, understandably, reluctant to confront Pharaoh, but the Lord promises to make him like God to Pharaoh, with Aaron as his prophet. Pharaoh himself was seen by his people as an intermediary between the gods and human beings; God is giving Moses superior status.

Again, Pharaoh is to be commanded to send the Israelites out of Egypt, but Moses is told that hard-hearted Pharaoh will not obey the Lord (vs 3,4). It is going to take a prolonged campaign, involving multiple miraculous signs, before the Israelites will be able to leave Egypt. This is not only to achieve the freedom of the Israelites, but so that the people of Egypt, with all their gods, will know that the Lord is supreme.

Pharaoh is not impressed. So, Aaron is instructed by the Lord to throw down his staff and it becomes a serpent (v 9). It is not Moses or Aaron who decide to perform a magic trick – this is the Lord's command.

Although the 'Egyptian magicians' can turn their staffs into snakes, Aaron's swallows theirs (v 12). There were many species of snake in Egypt, some very dangerous. Some of the Egyptian gods took the form of serpents; this demonstration put them in their place.

> 'And the Egyptians will know that I am the LORD when I stretch out my hand against Egypt and bring the Israelites out of it.'
>
> **Exodus 7:5**

## RESPOND

Paul says, 'We are therefore Christ's ambassadors, as though God were making his appeal through us' (2 Corinthians 5:20). Pray for opportunities to speak for him today.

........................................................................

**Bible in a year:** Judges 13,14;  Proverbs 7,8

# Water pollution

**PREPARE**
Pray that the Lord will make you teachable always.

**READ**
Exodus 7:14-24

**EXPLORE**
Lately, the newspapers have been full of stories of the pollution in Britain's rivers. Repeated warnings have been ignored and now life in the rivers is threatened. This is nothing compared with what happens to the river Nile when Pharaoh ignores God's command to send out the people of Israel. The mighty Nile is the secret of Egypt's wealth and power; a reliable source of water made agriculture possible in an otherwise arid part of the world. Making the water unusable is a devastating blow to Pharaoh's realm.

Some commentators have sought to find natural explanations for a change in the appearance of the river, but the passage makes clear that this was a sudden occurrence brought about by the action of Aaron at the Lord's command, even in stored water (v 19). Egyptian magicians are somehow able to duplicate the changing of water to blood, which will not have helped the situation (v 22).

Pharaoh refuses to listen to the Lord. His heart becomes harder, and he embarks on a battle of wills with the Lord.

The Egyptians are able to access clean water only by digging for it along the banks of the river, where no doubt the sand acts as a natural filter. Pharaoh simply retreats to his palace (v 23); he presumably has others to do the digging and bring him water.

> The fish in the Nile died, and the river smelled so bad that the Egyptians could not drink its water. Blood was everywhere in Egypt.
>
> **Exodus 7:21**

**RESPOND**
Do you know anyone who seems very resistant to the gospel? Pray for the Lord to soften their heart.

**Bible in a year:** Judges 15,16; Proverbs 9,10

# Shallow repentance

## PREPARE

**Pray, or sing: 'Change my heart, O God, Make it ever true; Change my heart, O God, May I be like you.'\***

## READ

**Exodus 9:13–35**

## EXPLORE

More disasters follow the turning of the Nile to blood (7:25 – 9:12). Pharaoh's heart is not softened by infestations of frogs, gnats and flies. Illness strikes Egyptian livestock; Egyptian citizens are covered in boils but Pharaoh still will not listen to Moses and Aaron.

Then comes a prolonged and deadly storm. Finally, Pharaoh seems to have learned his lesson. He tells Moses, 'This time I have sinned' (v 27). Previously he has refused to acknowledge the Lord, even when, after the plague of gnats, his own magicians told him, 'This is the finger of God' (8:19). Now he acknowledges that he is in the wrong and promises that if Moses asks the Lord to stop the hail the Israelites will be able to leave (vs 27,28).

But Pharaoh changes his mind again (vs 34,35)! Pharaoh will discover that his failure to change will lead to more displays of God's power in order to convince him to acknowledge the incomparable God (v 14) and allow God's people to worship him. Temporary repentance is not limited to Pharaoh. The prophets will later berate God's only people for coming to God in repentance that only lasts two or three days: 'Your love is like the morning mist, like the early dew that disappears' (Hosea 6:4).

> Then Pharaoh summoned Moses and Aaron. 'This time I have sinned,' he said to them. 'The LORD is in the right, and I and my people are in the wrong.'

**Exodus 9:27**

## RESPOND

Tell the Lord of any besetting sins, of which you repent, only to commit again. Ask him to soften your heart.

\*Eddie Espinosa, Mercy/Vineyard Publishing, © 1982

**Bible in a year:** Judges 17,18; Proverbs 11,12

# Worship prioritised

**PREPARE**

Pray with the psalmist, 'Open my eyes that I may see wonderful things in your law' (Psalm 119:18).

**READ**

**Exodus 10:21–29**

**EXPLORE**

Once again Pharaoh says the people can leave Egypt, only to change his mind after a plague of locusts is lifted (10:20). In response, the Lord covers Egypt in darkness, except the places where the Israelites live (v 23).

Pharaoh tries to negotiate with the Lord. He will allow the Israelite men, women and children to leave, but they must leave their flocks behind. Does Pharaoh think that they will be unable to survive without their flocks and return to Egypt? But Moses refuses because, without live animals, sacrifices to the Lord can not be made (vs 25,26). Pharaoh grudgingly offers to give part of what is demanded (v 24). But the Lord has revealed himself to Moses and the Israelites as the great 'I am' who will rescue them and accompany them on the journey to the Promised Land (3:15–17). Moses will not settle for a deal which allows them to escape but *not* worship the Lord.

Worship is the natural response to redemption. In his letter to the church in Rome, Paul spends 11 chapters explaining how the Lord, through Jesus, offers redemption to both Jews and Gentiles. In response he urges a life of service and worship.

> But Moses said, 'You must allow us to have sacrifices and burnt offerings to present to the LORD our God.'
>
> Exodus 10:25

**RESPOND**

How should we worship? 'Therefore, I urge you, brothers and sisters, in view of God's mercy, to offer your bodies as a living sacrifice, holy and pleasing to God – this is your true and proper worship' (Romans 12:1).

**Bible in a year:** Judges 19,20; Psalm 44

# Egypt cries out

## PREPARE

Worship the Son of God who 'is the image of the invisible God, the firstborn over all creation' (Colossians 1:15).

## READ

**Exodus 11:1–10**

## EXPLORE

'Israel is my firstborn son,' the Lord says when he calls and commissions Moses (4:22). Of all the people groups in the world, God chose the people of Israel to be a blessing to the world. The prophet Hosea will later link this status to the Exodus from Egypt (Hosea 11:1). The firstborn son was special in ancient societies and would be expected to continue the family name and family traditions.

Events are turning out just as the Lord predicted. Pharaoh repeatedly refuses to let the Israelite slaves leave Egypt, so the ultimate sanction will be used – the death of the firstborn sons of Egypt. While his position may have insulated Pharaoh from the worst effects of earlier plagues, this time the disaster hits the royal household as much as every other Egyptian family (v 5; 12:29,30). Meanwhile, the Israelite families are spared. The distress call of the Israelites began the dramatic intervention of the Lord (2:23); it will end with a great cry from the land of Egypt (12:30).

Even as Pharaoh refuses to be moved by Moses' demands, his servants are impressed. Ordinary Egyptians respect their Israelite neighbours (vs 2,3). Have you ever been surprised by the reaction of others when you have made a stand for your faith?

'There will be loud wailing throughout Egypt – worse than there has ever been or ever will be again.'

Exodus 11:6

## RESPOND

Pray that your beliefs and lifestyle may make an impact on your family, friends and colleagues, even those who disagree with you.

**Bible in a year:** Judges 21; Proverbs 13,14

# Brotherly love

## PREPARE
Give thanks for members of your family.

· · · · · · · · · · · · · · · · · · · · · · · · · · · · · · · · · · · · · · ·

## READ
Psalm 133

## EXPLORE
Sesame, rose, jasmine, cinnamon, neroli, benzoin, amber and orange blossom were added to oil sourced from olive groves at monasteries on the Mount of Olives to create the precious oil with which King Charles III was anointed at his coronation. The fragrance must have been overwhelming. Anointing with oil is an ancient symbol of blessing and consecration.

A very special fragranced oil was prepared and used to anoint Aaron, his sons and their descendants as priests (Exodus 30:22–33). This was a symbol of God's blessing and of their ordination; the oil made them holy. Unity between brothers is like this – fragrant and special to God. Although the psalm may have spoken originally about unity within natural families, it also speaks to us about the unity of Christian believers.

As a hospital chaplain, I often met patients who were more worried about

their family's problems than their own. Some would tell of adult children who had fallen out and did not speak to each other. If that causes distress to human parents, imagine how God must feel when his children do not get along.

Mountain dew brings refreshment and enables vegetation to grow (v 3). Unity among the household of God welcomes the blessing of growth and refreshment.

How good and pleasant it is when God's people live together in unity!
**Psalm 133:1**

## RESPOND
Is there any discord in your family? Is there anything you can do to bring healing? Is there a Christian brother or sister with whom you do not get on? What might you do to improve the relationship?

**Bible in a year:** Ruth 1,2;  Proverbs 15,16

# Others before self

Every four years we watch the modern Olympic Games. Corinth, in New Testament times, hosted the Isthmian Games every two years. For centuries the Greeks, and later Romans too, competed there for sport, music and poetry crowns. Corinth was a busy commercial centre and port city. Ideas flourished there, as did the practices of the pagan religions of Aphrodite, Isis and others.

The church in Corinth was a wonderful mix of people. They were very gifted, their worship was never dull and they loved the working of the Holy Spirit in their midst. Men and women, slave and free, Greek, Roman and Jew, all came together in the fellowship of Christ. The church was full of enthusiasm, but, like any other church, it was still vulnerable. The church's witness to Christ was in danger of being seriously compromised, and there was a lack of consideration for others which was leading to friction and divisions between Christians.

Paul wrote his 1 Corinthians letter to the church there probably just three years after founding the church. In the six chapters we shall be looking at, Paul patiently urges a practical love which puts others before self – a love that goes out of its way to respect and strengthen everyone in the church. Our readings finish with Paul's famous passage on love: 'Though I speak with the tongues of men and of angels...'

About the writer
**Roger Combes**

Roger has ministered in parishes in London, Cambridge and Hastings, and as an archdeacon in West Sussex. Now retired, he and his wife Christine live in Crawley with good views of planes from London-Gatwick. They have two daughters and one entertaining grandson.

# Love building others up

## PREPARE
**Think of the people your actions will affect today.**

## READ
**1 Corinthians 8:1–13**

## EXPLORE

The church in Corinth had its share of 'know-alls', who knew all the answers. The danger of such knowledge is that it leads to SHS: 'swollen head syndrome'. Better by far is love which nurtures the faith and confidence of others (v 1).

Corinth had many temples for the worship of mythical or pagan gods and idols. The temples also acted as communal eating places. People brought animals to be sacrificed to a particular 'god', and afterwards the meat was cooked and eaten. Imagine how torn a new Christian might feel, relishing their new life in Christ, only to be reminded of, and possibly tempted back into, the old murky world of pagan sacrifice every time they had a meal. Some felt they were compromising their obedience to Christ by eating meat that had been sacrificed to an idol.

How could these sincere believers keep a clear conscience? Stronger Christians needed to help them. *Not* by saying that temple food was harmless (though it was – it was just food, v 8), nor that an idol was nothing (though it was – only the Lord is God, vs 4–6). Better, they, who could eat temple meat with an untroubled conscience, should be prepared to alter their behaviour – perhaps avoiding meat themselves – so as not to trigger confusion for the more sensitive believer (v 13).

> If I have the gift of prophecy and can fathom all mysteries and all knowledge, ... faith that can move mountains, but do not have love, I am nothing.
> **1 Corinthians 13:2**

### RESPOND
**Have you recently had occasion to change your behaviour so as not to trigger a problem of conscience for someone else?**

**Bible in a year:** Ruth 3,4; Psalm 45

# The gospel free of charge

## PREPARE

Our access to God does not depend on who or what we are, but on his love. Pray: 'Thank you, Lord.'

## READ

**1 Corinthians 9:1–18**

## EXPLORE

As an apostle preaching the gospel, Paul was entitled to earn his living from it (vs 1–14). But he decided in Corinth to forgo this right (vs 12,15–18) so that he could present the gospel free of charge (v 18), as indeed it is.

He expected everyone to recognise that he was an apostle, and that it was legitimate for him to be sustained by his work like other workers. Soldiers, shepherds, farm labourers and temple priests (vs 7,13) all benefited from their work in cash or kind. Even animals were sustained as they worked (vs 8,9). Likewise, says Paul, an apostle can expect to be supported from the fruit of his labours (vs 10–12). Local churches today still have a responsibility to provide proper remuneration and support for their appointed leaders, teachers and employees (v 14).

Nevertheless, Paul renounced this right for himself in Corinth, because he felt that asking for money would hinder the gospel there (vs 12,18). He did not elaborate, but he was adamant that his priority was communicating the gospel of Christ. And if it would be helped by a sacrifice of his own, he was more than content. In fact, doing so was a matter of pride and deep satisfaction for him – his 'boast' and 'reward' (vs 15,18).

> Woe to me if I do not preach the gospel!
>
> **1 Corinthians 9:16**

## RESPOND

Is there a right or privilege you would willingly forgo if it might clear the way for the gospel to reach someone?

---

**Bible in a year:** 1 Samuel 1–3; Proverbs 17,18

# Adaptable and disciplined

## PREPARE
'One thing I ask from the LORD' (Psalm 27:4). What would that be for you today?

## READ
**1 Corinthians 9:19–27**

## EXPLORE
A scholarly Bible teacher was visiting a deprived area in the Philippines where small children were being cared for. The visitor was invited to speak to them, so he sat down with them and taught them to sing the old children's chorus: 'Two little eyes to look to God, two little ears to hear his Word...' (Anon). He was adapting his methods to win his audience.

Paul freely adapted his methods to suit the people he was among. When he was with Jews ('those under the law', v 20), he adopted their constraints. When he was with foreigners (v 21), he needed to be more flexible. Again, he would side with a diffident, hesitant person (v 22a), though he himself was outgoing and confident. All because he wanted to win all people to the unchanging gospel (v 22b).

Athletes dreaming of a medal know they must be disciplined as they train and compete. They must 'really want it', and exercise self-control. Paul says it is the same if we want to save others. We shall need determination (v 24), a focused aim (v 26) and the self-discipline (vs 25,27) to adjust our approach and respond to different people as may best save them. An eternal prize awaits (vs 25,27).

> I have become all things to all people so that by all possible means I might save some.
>
> **1 Corinthians 9:22**

## RESPOND
How flexible are we in the ways we attempt to reach various people with the gospel? Can we adapt as we reach out to people from different backgrounds?

**Bible in a year:** 1 Samuel 4–6; Proverbs 19,20

# Learning from our past

## PREPARE
'Offer your bodies as a living sacrifice ... pleasing to God' (Romans 12:1). Pray: 'Lord, how can I best please you today? Amen.'

## READ
**1 Corinthians 10:1–13**

## EXPLORE
In the TV series *Who Do You Think You Are?*, a celebrity is helped to delve into their genealogy and discover some of their heritage. The Corinthian Christians and Paul were family ('brothers and sisters'), and their spiritual ancestors were the children of Israel (v 1) whom God rescued from Egypt.

There was so much for the Corinthian Christians to learn from their heritage. Under Moses, God had blessed the family wonderfully. He had saved them, sustained them, watched over them and accompanied them (vs 2–4). But things had gone wrong too (vs 5–10). Some of their ancient predecessors had allowed misdirected desires to lead them into forbidden territory: idolatry, debauchery or immorality, with far-reaching consequences. 'God was not pleased' (v 5) – to put it mildly.

'These things ... were written down as warnings for us' (v 11), says Paul. The Corinthians, like their predecessors, had been much blessed. So beware! If we are blessed, we too can fall (v 12). Any Christian, however much respected or 'successful', can fall calamitously. No one is not tempted. But don't despair. God is faithful. He knows our limits. Look for the way out that God provides (v 13).

> ... God is faithful; he will not let you be tempted beyond what you can bear. But when you are tempted, he will also provide a way out so that you can endure it.
>
> **1 Corinthians 10:13**

## RESPOND
Imagining ourselves in the shoes of someone in the story can help us learn what the Lord is saying to us now. Keep this in mind as you read.

**Bible in a year:** 1 Samuel 7–9; Proverbs 21,22

# Which side are you on?

## PREPARE
**Pray not to be lured away from your wholehearted Christian commitment.**

## READ
**1 Corinthians 10:14–22**

## EXPLORE

In sport, you can usually tell which side a player is on from their shirt or the direction of their play. Though sometimes an 'own goal' or a bad mistake can make you wonder!

When we drink the wine and eat the bread in the Lord's Supper, we are showing ourselves to be stakeholders in the death and resurrection of Christ. We are taking part with his followers down the centuries (vs 15,16). The familiar words for this, such as 'fellowship', 'Communion' and 'sharing', need to be understood dynamically; like being a 'shareholder in', or being 'in solidarity with' Christ and his people. Receiving Communion in bread and wine is making a big statement of oneness with Christ's people (v 17).

Corinth in Paul's time would have staged lots of feasts and festivals with sacrifices to idols. So isn't this just harmless fun? An idol is nothing really, is it? Paul is definite. Active participation in such pagan sacrifice is a line not to be crossed (v 14). He gives three reasons:

- It can be dangerous for your spiritual life (v 20).

- Whose side are you on anyway? Partaking of Christ and partaking of idol worship are incompatible (v 21).

- You could be making the Lord actively jealous over your disloyalty (v 22).

Therefore, my dear friends, flee from idolatry.
**1 Corinthians 10:14**

## RESPOND

Are there aspects of your world which seem harmless enough, but it makes sense for someone on Christ's side to observe as lines not to be crossed? What are your lines?

**Bible in a year:** 1 Samuel 10,11; Psalms 46,47

# Seek the good of others

## PREPARE

Pray: 'Lord, give me "love, which comes from a pure heart and a good conscience and a sincere faith"' (1 Timothy 1:5).

## READ

**1 Corinthians 10:23 – 11:1**

## EXPLORE

'Please! Say yes!' There are many dilemmas in bringing up children. Parents worry about whether they're being too strict or too easy-going, too protective or too 'pushy'.

Life often poses dilemmas for Christians who are commendably involved in the secular world. How far should they go in adopting the practices of those around them? What guiding principles does Paul give the Christians in Corinth? Not sharing in the world's idolatry, obviously, as we saw yesterday (v 14). But, secondly, neither need they be over-scrupulous, actively searching out problems. 'The earth is the Lord's' (vs 25–27), and he means us to enjoy it! A third guiding principle is the faith or conscience of others. Paul is, in effect, saying: if what I do causes other believers to stumble in their faith, then I will not do it, even though my own conscience would allow me to do it (vs 28,29a,32).

This is a far-reaching principle, and it summarises much of the last three chapters. It is putting others first, seeking to build up the faith of others rather than seeking my own advantage or pleasure (vs 24,33b). This was the principle that Paul and Jesus followed, and we are called to follow it too (11:1).

No one should seek their own good, but the good of others.
1 Corinthians 10:24

## RESPOND

Has your conscience adjusted over time, allowing you more freedom in some areas and less in others? How do you react to someone whose Christian conscience is stricter (or more permissive) than yours?

**Bible in a year:** 1 Samuel 12,13;  Proverbs 23,24

# By night

'He who watches over you ... will neither slumber nor sleep' (Psalm 121:3,4).
Pray: 'Thank you, Lord, that you are always there for us.'

READ
**Psalm 134**

EXPLORE

We depend on many different people whose work is night work: nurses, care workers, doctors, people in emergency services, armed forces, transport, hospitality, manufacturing, security and many more. Some readers of these notes will be reading this before or after doing a night shift.

There was night work for the Levites working in the Temple (1 Chronicles 9:27,33; 23:28–30). Their tasks were various, not least continuing the praise of God day and night, as they had for centuries. This brief psalm was perhaps the Temple worshippers giving encouragement liturgically to the Levites on night duty (vs 1,2), and verse 3 was the Levites responding, assuring the congregation of the Lord's blessing on them as they headed home. Or perhaps it was a general act of fellowship that included everyone in the Temple. They turned to the Lord in praise, and believed the promise of his blessing, entrusting themselves to their faithful Creator at the end of the day.

How do you end the day? As the needle on a compass reverts to magnetic north when at rest, how good it is if our heart and mind can reset before sleep. A verse, a prayer or a page from a Christian book last thing at night can help us daily to rest in Christ.

May the Lord bless you from Zion, he who is the Maker of heaven and earth.

**Psalm 134:3**

RESPOND

Pray for any people you know whose work includes night work, that the Lord who never sleeps will give them alertness, compassion and resilience.

**Bible in a year:** 1 Samuel 14,15; Proverbs 25,26

# Women and men in worship

## PREPARE

Call to mind something to thank God for from church yesterday, or recently.

---

## READ

**1 Corinthians 11:2–16**

## EXPLORE

Presumably they understood this passage in Corinth, but it remains quite a mystery for us. Opinions differ widely, even among Bible-believing Christians, over how to understand Paul's teaching here, and even on the meaning of certain words: eg 'head' (v 3), 'covered' (vs 4,5), and 'angels' (v 10).

Verse 2 is fairly clear. Paul commends his readers for their praying and for staying faithful to the fundamentals of the faith that he passed on to them, eg the death and resurrection of Christ (see 15:3). Another clear point, headgear aside, is that Paul expected women to take part as men did in 'praying' and 'prophesying' (speaking for God?) in the church's worship together (vs 4,5).

Here is a further, very tentative, suggestion on the passage. Unlike Jewish men at prayer, Christian men prayed with their heads *uncovered*, to mark their freedom through Christ to enter God's presence. Maybe Christian women in Corinth wanted to mark their own equality and freedom in Christ in the same way, and were removing some kind of covering from their hair. While absolutely affirming women's equal freedom, Paul was perhaps saying that women who uncovered their hair were giving a quite different and undesirable impression in that social context. So perhaps he was urging them not to offend unnecessarily against the social proprieties of the day.

For as woman came from man, so also man is born of woman. But everything comes from God.

**1 Corinthians 11:12**

## RESPOND

How good are you at living with question marks, while holding to the fundamentals of the faith?

---

**Bible in a year:** 1 Samuel 16,17; Psalm 48

# The Lord's Supper or not?

## PREPARE
**Good Friday was over a month ago. Ponder its message again today.**

## READ
**1 Corinthians 11:17–34**

## EXPLORE

In a large house in Corinth, church members bring food for a meal before the Lord's Supper; but it gets out of hand. Some church members eat their nice food unaware of the needs of others, some drink too much, some are greedy leaving no food for those coming later, and some feel alone and second-class (vs 17–22). Although they are meeting for the Lord's Supper, they have lost sight of 'the body of Christ' (v 29), caring little about the magnitude of what happened on the cross, nor about the preciousness of being Christ's people together. It's a disgrace.

The very words of Jesus, 'This is my body … my blood', transport us back to the original Lord's Supper and the wonder of his sacrifice and victory (vs 23–25). Every time we take the bread and wine, we are preaching a little sermon to the world about the Lord (v 26), and giving a testimony that 'I am his and he is mine'.*

Worshipping God together is wonderful and necessary. The New Testament is clear that congregational worship needs self-discipline and some light-touch regulation; self-indulgence needs to be checked and everyone needs to feel welcome. At the Lord's table especially, we should accept one another. 'You should all eat together,' says Paul (v 33).

> In the same way, after supper he took the cup, saying, 'This cup is the new covenant in my blood; do this, whenever you drink it, in remembrance of me.'
>
> **1 Corinthians 11:25**

## RESPOND

'Take and eat this in remembrance that Christ died for you, and feed on him in your heart by faith with thanksgiving.'**

*AC Thistleton, *1 Corinthians Shorter Commentary*, Eerdmans, 2006, p191
**Book of Common Prayer*, adapted

**Bible in a year:** 1 Samuel 18,19;  Proverbs 27,28

# That's the Spirit

## PREPARE

Pray: 'May the blessing of God, Father, Son and Holy Spirit, be on me today. Amen.'

## READ

**1 Corinthians 12:1–11**

## EXPLORE

In those days it took great courage to say, 'Jesus is Lord'. It could be fatal to insist on it, or to refuse to say 'Caesar is Lord' at an emperor worship ceremony, for instance. This brave testimony, 'Jesus is Lord', came from the Holy Spirit (v 3), and it still does today across the world.

Some of the spiritual or supernatural activity in Corinth was pagan (v 2). But the Holy Spirit was active there in an amazing variety of ways, as he still is in a fellowship of believers today. Through the Spirit, the Lord gives each believer some gift for the good of all (vs 7,11). Opinions may vary as to what precisely Paul was referring to in the gifts he mentions at Corinth (vs 8–10). I always associate the popular author, CS Lewis, with having a gift of imparting 'knowledge', a gift which has greatly strengthened many Christians in the English-speaking world. James Hudson Taylor's gift of pioneering 'faith'

established a great enduring church work in South East Asia.

In your local church the same Holy Spirit is working through people he has gifted: perhaps, as in verses 8–10, someone can bring words of wisdom, someone else can speak from God, and others bring healing or discernment, or work wonders in all they do!

> Now to each one the manifestation of the Spirit is given for the common good.
>
> **1 Corinthians 12:7**

## RESPOND

Do you know what gift(s) the Holy Spirit has chosen to give you? Have you asked other Christians what *they* think your gift(s) might be?

**Bible in a year:** 1 Samuel 20–22; Proverbs 29,30

# Consider yourself well in

## PREPARE
Thank God for his greatest gift of all, Jesus Christ – Lord of all, Saviour and Friend.

## READ
**1 Corinthians 12:12–20**

## EXPLORE
Have you ever felt excluded by some Christians because you did not have the same gifts as them? Or have you ever wanted God to give you a particular gift which he has bestowed on someone else? Have you felt that you are not needed? Have you even tried to be a lone-ranger Christian, without the church?

Verse 13 is key. *All* believers in Jesus have been 'baptised by the Spirit into one body'. Each believer has been fully incorporated by the Holy Spirit into the one body, the church. Each believer is a part of the whole, and, like the different limbs and organs of a human body, every part is needed. We are the body of Christ (vs 12,27).

As in Corinth, a local church glorifies Christ by its diversity, being made up of believers who differ widely – ethnically, socially and in their abilities, gifts, personalities and experiences that God has given each one (vs 13,15–18). You may be the only person like you in your church; therefore you are especially needed! Those in the body of Christ who are disabled or suffering will reflect our Saviour in a way others do not. A church depends on all kinds of people using their various gifts faithfully and collaboratively.

> For we were all baptised by one Spirit so as to form one body – whether Jews or Gentiles, slave or free – and we were all given the one Spirit to drink.
>
> **1 Corinthians 12:13**

## RESPOND
Praise God for other people's gifts, both the apparently more 'supernatural' and the more 'ordinary'.

**Bible in a year:** 1 Samuel 23,24; Proverbs 31

# Say no to church rivalry

## PREPARE

Pray: 'Help me, Lord Christ, to love your body, the church, as you do. Amen.'

## READ

**1 Corinthians 12:21–31a**

## EXPLORE

A local church can be prone to 'division' (v 25), with some members at odds with others. A sense of self-importance or superiority (vs 21,22) can creep in, and rivalries or rifts soon emerge.

The answer is that we are each a different part of the body of Christ, and care for each other (vs 25–27). In the human body, each part depends on the others. The eye looks out for the hand, and the hand washes the foot. Obscure organs, the thyroid for instance, are also vital for the whole, and we show great respect for them too. So too in the body of Christ, all the members value and respect all the others, whatever role or gift God has allocated to each.

We do not choose who has which gifts. God distributes his gifts as he sees best (vs 4,11,18,24,28). His provision ranges (v 28) from the apostles' foundational witness through to those who administer and help the church's life; and from those who guide the church to the deeply personal, inarticulate praise/ prayer of 'speaking in tongues'. Paul might surely have listed many more gifts the Spirit gives the church through the people (eg music?).

Our calling is to seek the best (v 31) and work humbly together, each playing our part.

> Now you are the body of Christ, and each one of you is a part of it.
>
> **1 Corinthians 12:27**

## RESPOND

Don't leave it to church leaders to thank and value those whose gifts are less prominent. We can all express appreciation to those whose part may go unnoticed.

**Bible in a year:** 1 Samuel 25,26; Psalm 49

# A much better way

## PREPARE

'Come down, O Love divine, / Seek thou this soul of mine / and visit it with thine own ardour glowing; / O Comforter draw near.'*

. . . . . . . . . . . . . . . . . . . . . . . . . . . . . . . . . . . . . . . . . . . . . . . . . . . . . . . . . . . . . . . . . . .

## READ

**1 Corinthians 12:31b – 13:13**

## EXPLORE

This uplifting passage is quite testing for all Christians and churches. Are you a loving person, or irritable? When people cross you, are you loving, or rude? Can you wait patiently? Do you show kindness? Do you appreciate truth rather than 'spin'? Do you resent another's success? At church, are you quietly conceited or do you love others? Are you eager to support others and believe the best about them? Will you persevere to the end for others, as Paul and Jesus did? Verses 4–7 are justly famous. One inner city youth leader, who was greatly used by God, and had known much hardship in his life, found these verses difficult to read. 'It cuts me up,' he said.

Love, says Paul, is indispensable. Our achievements may be impressive, but without love we are nothing (vs 1–3). How much better (12:31b) that we apply love when we meet tensions in a church; for example, as in Corinth, over people's different gifts in a church, or some people's sensitive consciences. Putting others before self is a much better way.

One day, everything will be made clear, and we shall see things in perspective (vs 8–13). Many things will pass away. Even diamonds are not for ever. But love is.

Love is patient, love is kind. It does not envy, it does not boast, it is not proud.

**1 Corinthians 13:4**

## RESPOND

How important is kindness to you? How central is it to the gospel? What part should it play in our church worship and day-to-day living?

*after Bianco da Siena (died c1434), tr RF Littledale

. . . . . . . . . . . . . . . . . . . . . . . . . . . . . . . . . . . . . . . . . . . . . . . . . . . . . . . . . . . . . . . . . . .

**Bible in a year:** 1 Samuel 27,28; 1 Corinthians 1

# This is my song

## PREPARE

'Speak, O Lord, as we come to you / To receive the food of your holy Word / Take your truth, plant it deep in us; / shape and fashion us in your likeness.'*

## READ

**Psalm 135**

## EXPLORE

Singing is supposed to be good for us, and it's great to do it in praise of God. Whether or not we like a particular hymn or worship song, it is lovely ('pleasant', v 3) to sing about the Lord and the reputation he deserves (v 13).

So praise the Lord! This psalm writer does not hesitate to lift verses from other psalms (eg Psalms 134,115), to express how he has found that his God is incomparably great. The Lord is sovereign throughout his creation and unrivalled in his power (vs 5–7). His people are his choice possession, and he has famously intervened to save them from historical enemies. Their land was a gift from him, and their future is assured (vs 8–12,14). Do you have a way of recalling God's interventions that have been special to you?

Man-made gods, by contrast, are just metal constructions (vs 15–17). They have no life or vision. They do not listen or communicate. Verse 18 might suggest we will become like what we worship. We who worship Jesus Christ hope it is so!

The psalm ends by calling us, for the eleventh time, to praise the living Lord, who blesses his people (134:3) and dwells with them (v 21).

> For the LORD will vindicate his people and have compassion on his servants.

**Psalm 135:14**

## RESPOND

Sing out your praise, joining the praise of the worldwide church and all the company of heaven!

*Keith Getty and Stuart Townend, 'Speak, O Lord', © Thankyou Music Ltd, 2006

**Bible in a year:** 1 Samuel 29–31; 1 Corinthians 2

# Not your average prophet...

The well-known story of Jonah takes place during the reign of King Jeroboam 2nd of Israel (2 Kings 14:23–27) about 750 years before Jesus' birth. It's about one of God's prophets who tries to run away from God but finds he can't. No surprises there, but as we take a closer look, we'll see that there's much more to it than is immediately obvious.

God tells Jonah to travel to Nineveh and warn Israel's dreaded enemies, the barbaric Assyrians, that he will punish them for their wickedness. He wants them to have the chance to repent before it's too late. But, when they do so, Jonah isn't happy! Like Jonah, we may think there's no way that perpetrators of evil deserve God's mercy and we are reluctant to see them forgiven. However, Daniel 9:9 tells us that God accepts everyone who turns to him and asks for forgiveness: 'The LORD our God is merciful and forgiving, even though we have rebelled against him.'

Sadly, the Ninevites' repentance doesn't last. History repeats itself. About 150 years later, through the prophet Nahum, God warns the Assyrians – once again – of judgement to come. But they ignore God's message, so his justice prevails. Subsequently, in 612 BC, the brutal Assyrian regime is overthrown.

How can these events speak to us? Pray for fresh understanding of the character of God, and how he deals with people. Ask God to challenge you about ways you respond to him. For example, perhaps we are more like Jonah than we care to admit!

**About the writer**
**Sue Clutterham**

A former Local Mission Partner with Scripture Union, Sue enjoys writing and editing material that helps people of all ages to explore the Bible in creative ways. Free time includes walking, reading and watching crime thrillers, as well as outings with friends and family to local tea shops. Her favourite place in the world is a deserted beach.

# A stroppy prophet

## PREPARE
As you read this familiar story, ask God to give you a deeper understanding of his grace.

......................................................................................................

## READ
**Jonah 1:1–17**

## EXPLORE
God's instructions to Jonah are straightforward, but unprecedented. He tells him to deliver a short message of warning to Israel's worst enemies. Until this point, prophets have only been sent to God's people, and only incidentally to Gentiles! And why does God want to reach out to such a cruel and violent nation anyway, who deserve everything that's coming to them? Self-centred Jonah has other ideas! In verse 3 and again in verse 5, we read, 'But Jonah…' How can he possibly imagine that he can run away from God (Psalm 139:7–10)?

But God, rather than giving up on his disobedient, runaway prophet, intervenes.

He sends a violent storm. As a result, the boat Jonah boarded at Joppa is in danger of sinking. Meanwhile, Jonah sleeps below deck, much to the captain's annoyance! Eventually, Jonah is sacrificed to save the crew (v 12) and the sailors turn to God, whose timely, piscine provision means that Jonah doesn't drown. In verses 15 and 17, see how God's compassionate nature and power over creation overrule and everyone is saved. This event highlights God's amazing grace!

The word of the LORD came to Jonah.
**Jonah 1:1**

## RESPOND
Thank God for rescuing Jonah, and the sailors too! Pray about any seemingly hopeless situations known to you – perhaps those that seem beyond God's grace. Ask God to have mercy and intervene in his mighty power, just as he did with Jonah.

......................................................................................................

**Bible in a year:** 2 Samuel 1,2;  Psalm 50

## Tuesday 7 May
Jonah 2:1–10

# A prodigal prophet

### PREPARE
Have there been times when you have cried out to God in desperation? What happened?

### READ
**Jonah 2:1–10**

### EXPLORE
The image in verse 5 of Jonah with seaweed wrapped around his head makes me smile! However, his predicament is no laughing matter. Brought to his senses inside the belly of a big fish, Jonah cries out to God. After quoting from the book of Psalms – many of which he would know by heart – Jonah gratefully acknowledges God's saving power and turns to him for help (v 6). And God? He doesn't give up on Jonah. He rescues him from the consequences of his rebellion (v 10). In Jesus' parable of the prodigal son, there are clear parallels between Jonah and the errant younger brother, who also comes to his senses eventually (Luke 15:17–20).

Interestingly, in Matthew 12:40, Jesus refers to Jonah and uses this event to illustrate his own forthcoming death and resurrection. As a result of Jesus' sacrifice, God listens to *our* cry, brings *us* up from the depths, and saves *us*!

And, although we may not always realise it, God rescues us time and time again. Check out Psalm 25:20. How great is our God! He meets us where we are and we can experience his power at work in our lives, as Jonah does.

'In my distress I called to the LORD, and he answered me.'
**Jonah 2:2**

### RESPOND
Where do you need to see God at work in your life? Is there anything from which you need to be rescued? Thank God for his saving power and call out to him – for yourself, or perhaps someone known to you.

**Bible in a year:** 2 Samuel 3–5; 1 Corinthians 3

# An obedient prophet

## PREPARE

Is there anything – large or small – that is stopping you doing what God wants? As we read today of the second chance God gave Jonah, ask him to reveal stuff that you may need to deal with, so that you can follow him wholeheartedly.

## READ

**Jonah 3:1–10**

## EXPLORE

Initially, God called out to Jonah, and Jonah ignored him (1:1–3). But when Jonah calls out to God, he gets a response (2:10)! At last, Jonah is ready to be obedient and is graciously given another opportunity (vs 1,2).

So, off he sets on the 500-mile journey to Nineveh to deliver God's message of warning to the Assyrian people. Nineveh was the capital of the Assyrian Empire, and at that time, around 750 BC, the largest and richest city in the world. But it was also a corrupt, cruel and evil regime – the modern-day equivalent of a terrorist state.

God's short message of warning through Jonah hits home. The outcome is amazing. The Ninevite people believe what God is saying and respond in repentance (v 5). Not only that – the king repents too! He even includes livestock in the resulting proclamation that everyone should cover themselves in sackcloth and turn from their evil ways (vs 6–9). How amazing it would be if we could see such a response to God today in our depraved world.

Jonah obeyed the word of the LORD.
**Jonah 3:3**

## RESPOND

Bring to God someone you know who desperately needs to meet with him. Ask God to show them his mercy and grace… and keep praying!

**Bible in a year:** 2 Samuel 6,7; 1 Corinthians 4

# A jealous prophet

## PREPARE

How would you feel if the ruthless dictator of a modern, evil regime were overthrown? How would you feel if they were soundly converted? Be honest!

## READ

**Jonah 4:1–11**

## EXPLORE

As with the rest of Jonah's story, this final part is all about God and his compassion, mercy and justice (3:10). Jonah, however, is furious that God has spared the Ninevites the punishment they deserve (v 1)! This time, his attitude mirrors that of the other, older brother in Jesus' story of the prodigal son. He's angry, jealous and resentful. Jonah now has a run-in with God, just as the firstborn son berates his father when his repentant brother returns home (Luke 15:28–32). Both scenarios end with a question, emphasising God's sovereign authority and supreme grace towards the lost, whether an individual (Luke 15:32) or a city of 120,000 people (verse 11).

Are we guilty of behaving like Jonah sometimes – perhaps in our attitude towards neighbours, colleagues, or even friends and family (James 4:12)? God teaches Jonah about his grace, first through a fish and then through a plant.

We are not told how Jonah responds at the end of the story, but at this point he seems unable to accept that God knows best.

'… you are a gracious and compassionate God, slow to anger and abounding in love, a God who relents from sending calamity.'

Jonah 4:2

## RESPOND

Rather than being about Jonah and a great big fish, this book is all about a great big God! Look back over Jonah's story. Reflect on how God's mercy and grace shine through the chaos. Thank God for the way he was at work through Jonah, despite his failings.

**Bible in a year:** 2 Samuel 8–10; 1 Corinthians 5

# God's hatred of evil

## PREPARE
The book of Nahum has no 'feel-good factor'. As we read more doom and gloom, reflect on what it teaches us about God.

. . . . . . . . . . . . . . . . . . . . . . . . . . . . . . . . . . . . . . . . . . . . . . . . . . . .

## READ
**Nahum 1:1–15**

## EXPLORE
Little is known of Nahum, who has the task of bringing God's strong judgement to Nineveh – again! Only about 100 years after their repentance in response to God's message through Jonah, the Assyrians have slipped back into their evil ways. God's anger at their behaviour is clear.

God leaves the recipients of his message in no doubt at all as to who has ultimate power – a comfort to us as we observe the current state of our world in the twenty-first century. And verse 7 brings comfort to the people of Judah, dominated by the cruel Assyrian regime. Verses 8 and 9 make it clear God will not allow the nation of Assyria to continue. The destruction of Nineveh (in 612 BC) is still in the future, so for the people of Judah this prophecy is an encouragement that, one day, their suffering will come to an end.

When confronted with Almighty God, human power is futile. Through Nahum, God asserts his authority (see in particular vs 2,3,6). God is righteous and holy and we can be confident that he is in control and justice will prevail (v 15).

> The LORD is slow to anger but great in power.
>
> **Nahum 1:3**

## RESPOND
Verse 7 brings hope – a reminder that we need to trust in God, whatever is happening. Easy to say, but hard to do! Read the verse again as a prayer for help and strength.

. . . . . . . . . . . . . . . . . . . . . . . . . . . . . . . . . . . . . . . . . . . . . . . . . . . .

**Bible in a year:** 2 Samuel 11,12;  Psalm 51

# Almighty and everlasting God

## PREPARE

You may be feeling drained after this week of evil versus good! The books of Jonah and Nahum are uncomfortable reading, and there's more to come today. Praise God that he has the ultimate victory, and the power and the glory are his.

## READ

**Nahum 2:1–13; 3:18,19**

## EXPLORE

God's message is for his people, the Israelites, but it's about their enemies, the Assyrians. Nineveh was at the heart of the Assyrian Empire. Through Jonah, God had graciously given the Ninevites a chance to repent, and they had responded.

However, it didn't last, and they returned to their evil ways. The subsequent years expose their shallow repentance – it's as though they had never turned to God. Now it's too late – they have sealed their own fate (3:19). There's no escape from God's judgement and their supposedly all-powerful regime is at an end, probably about 150 years after Jonah's original prophecy. The consequences of their actions are described in graphic detail. God's wrath, provoked by wickedness, is terrible (1:2,6).

Through these events, the two sides of God's nature are revealed – his care and compassion for his people (1:7; 2:2) and his hatred of evil and the subsequent consequences of wicked behaviour (1:2,3). Like Jonah, we cannot escape God, who will ultimately punish all evil (Revelation 11:18). But the good news in all this is that those of us who have responded to God's saving grace through Jesus (John 3:16) can look forward to his return one day. Come, Lord Jesus!

> Nineveh is like a pool whose water is draining away.
>
> **Nahum 2:8**

## RESPOND

Thank God for his ultimate victory over sin through Jesus and the promise he gives of eternal life with him for ever (Revelation 21:3–5)!

**Bible in a year:** 2 Samuel 13,14; 1 Corinthians 6

# Give thanks!

## PREPARE

If ever you need reminding that God's love is everlasting, then this is your psalm! Pray that, as you read it, you will be challenged and encouraged as you consider who God is, and what he has done to show us his great love.

## READ

**Psalm 136:1–26**

## EXPLORE

In Jewish tradition this psalm, intended for congregational singing, is known as the Great Psalm of Praise (*Hallel* in Hebrew). Like Psalm 135, this joyful prayer of praise and thanksgiving has repetitive phrases which emphasise again and again the nature and character of God. We recognise his goodness and sovereignty with thankfulness (vs 1–3), before reflecting on all that he has made, and done. The psalm concludes with reference to all that God continues to do as he meets our needs (vs 23–25).

So, we see the God of heaven as our creator (vs 4–9), rescuer (vs 10–16) and victor throughout history (vs 17–22), working miraculously to bring about his purposes. Why? Because of his steadfast and never-ending love for us. How tragic that the Ninevites, having turned to God in response to his message through Jonah, face his wrath and judgement when they subsequently reject him and the great love he offers them, despite their wickedness.

This is our opportunity to praise Almighty God, who has reigned supreme throughout history, but also cares for us and loves us for ever. Hallelujah!

His love endures for ever.

**Psalm 136:1**

## RESPOND

Read through this psalm again slowly, and aloud if possible. Pause every few verses to give thanks to God.

**Bible in a year:** 2 Samuel 15,16; 1 Corinthians 7

# The Bible and me –
## a writer's experience of the Bible

In these Spotlight articles we ask *Daily Bread* writers to tell us a little about what the Bible means to them. For this issue we talked with **Ro Willoughby**.

**What was your early experience of the Bible?**

I loved Jesus from as far back as I can remember. After breakfast my family read the Bible and we prayed. I loved Bible stories. I learned Bible verses by heart. The Bible told me how to live ... but, apparently, not how to think. At secondary school we debated the theories of evolution. I quoted from Genesis. My classmates looked mystified. To them the Bible was irrelevant. What could I say?

**How did your appreciation of the Bible grow as you got older?**

Going away to university, I intended to work out how far my Christian faith was simply a result of my upbringing. I was studying history – and history is about examining the evidence. So, I set about looking at the evidence for Jesus' resurrection. Probably, for the first time, I began to interrogate scripture. Whatever the outcome, it would be significant.

I read the last chapters of each Gospel again and again with two questions in my mind. Did this really happen? Does it matter? Within weeks I was convinced Jesus died, but then gloriously arose to new life. The Bible could withstand intellectual interrogation. There were reasons for Christian faith. I wanted to discover more.

I joined Bible study groups, listened to Bible readings in the Christian Union and sermons in church. I memorably heard John Stott say, 'The Bible is like a prescription. It can't make you better, but is the route to medicine that can.'

I went on to work with Christian students, encouraging them to study the Bible with other students searching for God. One dark evening I was leading such a study, reading about Jesus walking on the water. 'Imagine you're there,' I said. Suddenly I was rocking in the boat, hearing the wind howl, feeling spray on my face. My imagination, inspired by the Spirit, was taken into that story in a way that had never happened before. I saw Jesus with the eyes of my heart.

**How did becoming a parent affect your Bible reading?**

At London Bible College my understanding of God and his Word expanded, clothed in more richly coloured layers – and I met my husband. The year after our second child was born, I was so, so tired I rarely studied the Bible. But I remembered Bible verses and Bible stories. For several weeks, I inhabited one story, imagining myself there, rereading the stories to notice fresh details. I walked with Naomi and Ruth from Moab to Bethlehem, or with Mary visiting Elizabeth, and watched Jesus in the home of Simon the Pharisee.

We loved discovering the Bible with our children. We drew pictures (once of Saul falling on his sword!). We acted out stories. We learned psalms. We made a burning bush. For many years I edited Scripture Union's Bible reading material for junior-aged children, committed to helping them ask questions of the Bible and meet God as they did so.

Years later, I engaged with the Ignatian Spiritual Exercises. This took many months. No need to hurry, just spend time with God,

embraced in his love, immersed in scripture. This deepened my desire to be with him.

**And what about now?**

With my heart, I continue to experience Jesus' love on my own, and through others in my Bible study group, appropriately named for Sheffield, 'United on Wednesday'.

With my imagination, I marvel at the mystery of God. My husband's death in 2018 propelled me to reconsider the wonder of Jesus' resurrection, the nature of his resurrection body and metaphors and images in scripture that enlarge understanding of life with Christ beyond the grave.

With my mind I continue to know more of God. Living on my own, I have time to read, write, study and to chat with him. I have many opportunities to preach, opening up God's Word to those who are listening. My grandchildren love to hear me retell Bible stories!

The Holy Spirit gives me many fresh insights. This amazes me. Why have I never thought like this before?! Or have I forgotten? The truth is, the Bible is not just a prescription, but an ever-revealing kaleidoscope or maybe an ever-present magnet that goes on drawing me closer to God.

*Ro Willoughby*

# 'Come, Holy Spirit...'

About the writer
**Gethin Russell-Jones**

Gethin is the minister of Ararat Baptist Church, Cardiff. He is also a runner, podcaster, therapist, writer, occasional singer, husband, dad and grandad.

The Acts of the Apostles is widely regarded as the sequel to the Gospel of Luke. The author is referred to as the 'dear friend' and 'doctor' (Colossians 4:14), as well as being one of the apostle Paul's longest-serving travelling companions (2 Timothy 4:11). More than anything, Luke is a highly skilled writer who uses a variety of styles. Around the midpoint in Acts (16:10) things change. He shifts from speaking in the third person plural (they) to the first person plural (we). He becomes an embedded reporter, narrating events as an active participant and not simply a witness. Luke is an activist.

The ongoing presence of the Holy Spirit is one of Luke's dominant themes. In his Gospel we see him at work in the ministry of Jesus, ending with Jesus promising his followers that they too will be clothed with power from on high (Luke 24:49). Acts begins with Jesus repeating the injunction to wait in Jerusalem until they receive the Holy Spirit (1:4,5). The pivotal moment between the promise and the fulfilment is the ascension (Acts 1:9), where Jesus returns to the Father. On the day of Pentecost, the Spirit falls on the emerging Christian community and fills them with the Holy Spirit. He inspires Peter's proclamation and energises the new faith community. Luke is showing us that the same Spirit who was at work in Jesus is now present in the church.

# Power on

## PREPARE

Solar power harvests energy from the sun, turning it into power we can use. Jesus gives his followers a vision of Christian living that is charged with the presence of God on the inside. Pray: 'Lord, empower me today.'

## READ

**Acts 1:1–11**

## EXPLORE

The ancient site of Stonehenge in the west of England is still shrouded in mystery. Its stone circle and burial chamber, composed of bluestone rocks, was somehow transported from west Wales and was on its present site thousands of years before the birth of Christ. Part of an elaborate religious system, it is aligned to make the most of the earth's rotation around the sun. Jesus speaks here of an alignment that is needed in his disciples' lives. He has already told them not to leave Jerusalem once he has left them (1:4) but to wait for a gift from God.

The Holy Spirit's dynamic presence will effect change within the lives of his followers and also across the world. God's power begins on the inside and works through the whole of creation. Broken by bereavement and then bewildered by the hope of his resurrection, their lives are soon to be transformed by a new power. Armed with this dynamic and elemental power, they will become living witnesses to God's unfolding story.

'But you will receive power when the Holy Spirit comes on you; and you will be my witnesses in Jerusalem, and in all Judea and Samaria, and to the ends of the earth.'

**Acts 1:8**

## RESPOND

Pray: 'Lord, I thank you for this gift of power and I align myself to your loving purposes. May the light of your Spirit illumine my ways and help me be a living signpost to your kingdom.'

**Bible in a year:** 2 Samuel 17,18; Psalms 52–54

# One of us

## PREPARE

Call to mind people who were once close to you, but are not any more: there may now be awkwardness, avoidance and pain. Pray: 'Lord, have mercy on me and those with whom I once shared my life.'

## READ

**Acts 1:12–26**

## EXPLORE

A sensational autobiography by a member of the royal family accuses others within his family of conducting media briefings against him and his wife. Betrayal. Judas Iscariot's name is synonymous with going behind Jesus' back. He is one of the most troubling and fascinating characters in the Bible. His act of betrayal by making a deadly deal with the Jewish authorities is well known. And the 'Judas kiss' in the Garden of Gethsemane has a cultural resonance way beyond the pages of the Gospels (Luke 22:47,48). He is portrayed as a man doomed by his own choices and Jesus comments that it would have been better if he had not been born.

But there is another side. He was one of the original apostles, appointed by Jesus (Luke 6:16), and Peter here refers to him as 'one of us', who had a personal stake in their shared ministry. And yet it all went badly wrong. Even though Judas later shows remorse for his actions (Matthew 27:3,4), he is for ever remembered as a guilty man.

> 'He was one of our number and shared in our ministry.'
>
> **Acts 1:17**

## RESPOND

Pray: 'If I'm truthful, Lord, I can see myself in Judas. There have been periods when I have been full of faith, but plenty of others when my loyalty has been torn. I turn back to you now.'

**Bible in a year:** 2 Samuel 19,20;  1 Corinthians 8

# All together now

## PREPARE

Give thanks for your faith community and the love that is shared there. Remember those who lead, serve and help to build it up. Pray that unity might flourish and that it might be a place of healing.

## READ

**Acts 2:1–21**

## EXPLORE

Many Christian traditions include versions of an ancient piece of call-and-response liturgy in their Communion service. It begins with 'Lift your hearts', to which comes the reply, 'We lift them to the Lord'. During this exchange between the minister and the congregation, the minister says that we should give thanks and praise to God at all times and in all places. These words are ringing in my ears as I think about today's reading.

This fragile Christian community are all together and in one place, focused on the presence of God. As Jews, they gathered to celebrate the feast of Pentecost, six weeks after the Passover. They experienced the pain of grief and then the elation of the resurrection. Betrayal was uncovered and other relational tensions revealed. Jesus has ascended and they are once again left without his presence. But here they are, committed to each other and to the Lord with open hearts. And in obedience to him, they are waiting for a new power to grip them.

> When the day of Pentecost came, they were all together in one place.
>
> Acts 2:1

## RESPOND

Pray: 'Come, Holy Spirit, fill the hearts of your faithful and kindle in them the fire of your love. Send forth your Spirit and they shall be created. And you will renew the face of the earth.'*

*Catechism of the Catholic Church, paragraphs 2670–2672

**Bible in a year:** 2 Samuel 21,22; 1 Corinthians 9

# Thursday 16 May
## Acts 2:22–28

# The death of death

## PREPARE

Take a moment to listen to the rhythms of your breath, in and out. Feel your heart beating and be aware of the sights, smells and sounds around you. Remember you are held by God's love.

## READ

**Acts 2:22–28**

## EXPLORE

Winston Churchill is alleged to have said, 'I am prepared to meet my Maker. Whether my Maker is prepared for the great ordeal of meeting me is another matter.' It's a quote whose ready wit brings a smile to my face and yet it masks a real fear. Across the ages, people of all cultures and faith have been vexed about the meaning of life and death, especially the finality of death and our fragile mortality. While the religious mind looks for hope beyond the grave, many others seek consolation in living intentionally in the present moment. Death makes us uncomfortable.

Peter's short sermon on the day of Pentecost (only 22 verses) asserts the death of death in the death of Christ. Death itself has been vanquished in the resurrection. It's a note of triumph heard loudly in Paul's writings: 'Where,

O death, is your victory? Where, O death, is your sting?' (1 Corinthians 15:55). God's action in raising Jesus from the dead is good news for all humanity. Death no longer has the last laugh.

'But God raised him from the dead, freeing him from the agony of death, because it was impossible for death to keep its hold on him.'
**Acts 2:24**

## RESPOND

Find some stillness and listen once again to your breathing. You are mortal but held by One who is victorious over death, the grave and fear itself.

**Bible in a year:** 2 Samuel 23,24; 1 Corinthians 10

# Both Lord and Christ

## PREPARE
One writer has said that Christianity is the only faith to assert that the God who is with us is the God with scars. Jesus understands the depth of human pain. Turn to him now with yours.

## READ
**Acts 2:29–36**

## EXPLORE
In his well-known hymn, 'God Moves in a Mysterious Way', the troubled eighteenth-century writer William Cowper pens this verse:

*His purposes will ripen fast,*
*Unfolding ev'ry hour.*
*The bud may have a bitter taste,*
*But sweet will be the flow'r.*

Cowper is urging us, in worship, to recognise that God is able to bring hope out of the most adverse of circumstances. And the Bible is full of such assurances. I think of Joseph's early experiences as recorded in the book of Genesis – a catalogue of injustice and betrayal. Reflecting on his life, he says to his brothers: 'You intended to harm me, but God intended it for good' (Genesis 50:20).

It's an idea that resonates in the climax to Peter's sermon, that this Jesus who was crucified has now been exalted to the highest place. Commenting on verse 36, Joseph A Fitzmyer suggested that, by referring to him as Lord, Peter is elevating Jesus to the same status as God (v 36). This is the holiest name that can be given to Jesus.

'Therefore let all Israel be assured of this: God has made this Jesus, whom you crucified, both Lord and Messiah.'

**Acts 2:36**

## RESPOND
Come before God with all your disappointments and regrets, asking that you might know his hope, even as you process difficult feelings. Pray: 'Lord, assure me that you are at work even when all seems hopeless.'

**Bible in a year:** 1 Kings 1,2; Psalm 55

Acts 2:37–41

# The gift of life

## PREPARE

Pray: 'I come before the Lord, the giver of life. The One who hovered over the face of the deep, whose breath is in our lungs. I come in need of the renewal of my life. Lord, breathe in me again.'

## READ

**Acts 2:37–41**

## EXPLORE

There's a news story in a national newspaper today, about declining church attendance. According to a Church of England report, church attendance has fallen more than 20 per cent since the pandemic. Strangely, it blames a lack of supply of church services, rather than a lack of demand from worshippers. In a climate of long-term church decline in Europe, it's hard to engage with the sermon finale in today's reading (v 41). There's an urgency in this account that seems a world away from our reality today.

Peter's sermon has reached its climax. Moved by his presentation of the life, death, resurrection and exaltation of Jesus, the crowd is torn open by his words (v 37). We hear their emotional plea: 'What shall we do?' And Peter answers by emphasising four key elements of salvation: repentance, baptism, forgiveness of sins and receiving the Holy Spirit. The responses required are specific and sequential. Some scholars see here a pattern of Christian initiation that can be seen throughout Acts. And the Spirit who brings the church to life and energises its mission is also promised to individuals.

> When the people heard this, they were cut to the heart and said to Peter and the other apostles, 'Brothers, what shall we do?'
>
> **Acts 2:37**

## RESPOND

Pray using the words of Daniel Iverson's hymn: 'Spirit of the living God, fall afresh on me. Spirit of the living God, fall afresh on me.'

**Bible in a year:** 1 Kings 3–5; 1 Corinthians 11

# The life of God within

## PREPARE

Pray: 'Lord, on this special day, I remember that your love holds me. In you I live and move and have my being.* Your holy presence is within me.' Pause to reflect on this staggering truth.

## READ

John 14:15–27

## EXPLORE

One Sunday evening, many moons ago, I was preaching on a verse in Paul's letter to the Galatians where he speaks about the presence of the Holy Spirit, saying he is within us, crying out, *Abba*, or Daddy (Galatians 4:6). The penny dropped for me as I read these words. For the first time, I realised that worship is something in which I participate *with* God. There is an infinite flow of love going on within God and, through Christ, I am drawn into this circle of praise.

Jesus' words here are similarly mind-boggling. His friends will soon realise they are intimately attached with the life of God. Henry Scougal (1650–78), a young Scottish theologian who died in his twenties, wrote a short book with an arresting title: *The Life of God in the Soul of Man*. At one point, he writes, 'Christians know by experience that true religion is a union of the soul with God, a real participation in the divine nature, the very image of God drawn upon the soul…'

'On that day you will realise that I am in my Father, and you are in me, and I am in you.'

John 14:20

## RESPOND

Pause to be still. Become mindful of your own presence but also of another within. Pray: 'Lord, help me know your intimacy in the depth of my being.'

*Acts 17:28

**Bible in a year:** 1 Kings 6,7; 1 Corinthians 12

# A radical vision

## PREPARE

In a culture obsessed with social media and celebrity, seek the simplicity of God's stillness. Find a quiet place and whisper the 'Jesus prayer': 'Lord Jesus Christ, Son of God, have mercy on me, a sinner.'

- - - - - - - - - - - - - - - - - - - - - - - - - - - - - - - - - - - - - - - - - -

## READ

**Acts 2:42–47**

## EXPLORE

A long time ago, in the summer I sat my A levels, I joined a Christian street theatre company for a few weeks. The company hailed from St Michael le Belfry, York, a church renowned for its creativity in mission. That summer, however, we were based in a well-known seaside resort in the north-west of England. Each day we performed in the town's parks, promenade, hotels and seafront. By night we retired to the church where we lived together, in different rooms and halls. We pooled our money to buy food and refreshments; we worshipped and learned together before going out into the town. I felt like we held everything in common for those few weeks. As an 18-year-old, it was intoxicating. I get the same feeling as I read this passage in today's reading.

Here we see the earliest Christian community, gathering around a shared life, and the four distinct elements mentioned in verse 42: the apostles' teaching, fellowship, the breaking of bread and prayer. Everything is held in community, for the community and for others.

> They devoted themselves to the apostles' teaching and to fellowship, to the breaking of bread and to prayer.
>
> Acts 2:42

## RESPOND

Think of the communities with whom you share your life, love and faith. Thank God for seeing the risen Christ at work there.

- - - - - - - - - - - - - - - - - - - - - - - - - - - - - - - - - - - - - - - - - -

**Bible in a year:** 1 Kings 8,9;  Psalms 56,57

# Money can't buy you love

Think of the times when your presence has been noticed: feelings of being seen by others and respected, of trust and belonging. Thank God for these occasions. Pray: 'Lord, help me make others feel special too.'

READ

**Acts 3:1–10**

EXPLORE

I was once a part-time hospital chaplain, visiting the cottage hospital once a week and making my way around all the wards. On one occasion, a lady asked me to pray for her as she had suffered a nasty fall. It was a hurried prayer as I was busy. Some months later, there came a series of loud knocks on the church office door. There she stood, beaming, saying that she had been healed and could walk freely, something she had been unable to do for years.

Peter and John's plans have been disturbed here. As Jewish believers, it was their practice to take part in Temple prayers, three times a day. This story highlights the profound changes that have taken place since the day of Pentecost. The Holy Spirit came upon the new community of faith, inspired Peter's sermon and stimulated an extraordinary response in his listeners.

The Spirit's presence is now evident in the healing of this disabled man. The Spirit is still everywhere.

> They recognised him as the same man who used to sit begging at the temple gate called Beautiful, and they were filled with wonder and amazement at what had happened to him.
>
> Acts 3:10

RESPOND

Pray: 'God, forgive me that I often live as a self-sustaining Christian. I get by on my good words and deeds. Open my eyes to your Spirit's power, presence and availability in all times and places.'

**Bible in a year:** 1 Kings 10,11; 1 Corinthians 13

## Wednesday 22 May
### Acts 3:11–26

# Refreshing faith

## PREPARE

Pray: 'It's been a while, Lord, since I felt refreshed by your presence. I feel I'm going through the motions too often in my spiritual life. I open my heart to you now and ask for times of refreshing once again.'

## READ

**Acts 3:11–26**

## EXPLORE

Many scholars have identified a pattern in the sermons found in the early chapters of Acts:

- Jesus is the longing expressed by prophets (v 18)...

- fulfilled in his life, ministry, death and resurrection, and now...

- exalted to God's right hand as Lord (v 21). The Holy Spirit's presence...

- is the sign of Christ's reign and this will be consummated...

- when he returns as Lord of all and...

- an appeal is then made with the offer of forgiveness and salvation.

Inherent in Peter's sermon is an invitation to his fellow Jews to be refreshed in their faith (v 19), that the breath of God, coming from his presence, might reinvigorate them. Jesus is introduced not as the last in a long line of great heroic figures but as God's presence among his people.

This calls for a complete about-turn on our part and not simply a readjustment in our thinking.

'Repent, then, and turn to God, so that your sins may be wiped out, that times of refreshing may come from the Lord.'

Acts 3:19

## RESPOND

Pray: 'Lord, open the eyes of my heart that I might see Jesus clearly again. May I see him more clearly, love him more dearly and follow him more nearly, day by day.'*

*after Richard, Bishop of Chichester, 1197–1253

**Bible in a year:** 1 Kings 12,13; 1 Corinthians 14

# I've got the power

## PREPARE

What are the dominant voices in your life? Come now to hear the whisper of God's Spirit in the Bible. Not in the earthquake, wind or fire, but in his still small voice (1 Kings 19:12), calling you to himself.

## READ

**Acts 4:1–12**

## EXPLORE

A regular flow of disturbing news stories in the UK is rocking confidence in a number of police forces. Many people are wondering how this will affect the public's relationship with the police. Under the UK's unwritten constitution, policing is by consent of the public. Police officers are just ordinary citizens who have been given authority to preserve law and order. Once their good name is questioned, public confidence in their authority is eroded.

In this story, the question of authority is slung at Peter and John. By what name and power are they preaching and performing these miracles (v 7)? For Peter and John's listeners, authority lay with the priests, Temple guards and Sadducees (v 1). But with careful precision, Luke describes the moment between the question and Peter's answer. Peter is filled with the Holy Spirit (v 8). This is the answer to the question. These men are flooded with the power of God. This is their badge of authority.

> They had Peter and John brought before them and began to question them: 'By what power or what name did you do this?'
>
> Acts 4:7

## RESPOND

Pray: 'As I seek to be a faithful follower of Jesus, loving others and open to the Spirit, may I too know God's good pleasure in my life as I demonstrate the good news in my words and actions.'

**Bible in a year:** 1 Kings 14,15;  1 Corinthians 15

# Illiterate and ignorant

## PREPARE

This is a time to be with Jesus. He is with us all the time and in all places. Pause now to focus on his astonishing promise: 'I am with you always, to the very end of the age' (Matthew 28:20).

## READ

**Acts 4:13–22**

## EXPLORE

Once, at a party, I stood with two very eminent doctors – and there was I, a struggling freelance PR consultant! I chuckled at the thought that I was a spin doctor among physicians. I felt intimidated by their intellectual achievements, even though they were both humble and self-effacing. Comparing ourselves to others is always a joyless endeavour and this reading exposes the flaw in our attempts to be at the top of the pecking order.

Faced with Peter and John's persuasive words and stunning miracles, I can hear the scorn in the religious leaders' put-down. These men are illiterate and ignorant (v 13)! What have they got to offer us? And they had a point. It's highly likely that neither of them could read or write and they were utterly unfamiliar with the rhetorical skills of the Temple. And yet their critics noted that they had been with Jesus. The indisputable power at work in their lives was apparent for all to see. If nothing else, the healed man was still there (v 14), a living testimony to the power of the risen Christ.

> When they saw the courage of Peter and John and realised that they were unschooled, ordinary men, they were astonished and they took note that these men had been with Jesus.
>
> **Acts 4:13**

## RESPOND

Pray with Paul the apostle in these famous words: 'But whatever were gains to me I now consider loss for the sake of Christ' (Philippians 3:7).

**Bible in a year:** 1 Kings 16,17; Psalms 58,59

# Crying out loud

## PREPARE

How do you react to trouble when it comes? Are you driven towards God or away from him? Pray: 'Lord, I'm familiar with both directions and I ask that you would help me turn to you in my next crisis.'

## READ

**Acts 4:23-31**

## EXPLORE

It was the largest prayer meeting I'd ever attended. It was a Wednesday morning in Seoul, South Korea. I expected a small gathering and was totally overwhelmed. There were 5,000 people present, including a choir and orchestra. After the pastor gave a short sermon and we'd recited the Lord's Prayer and Apostles' Creed, he invited the congregation to pray. Not silently, or in small groups, or even one after another. We were to pray out loud, in our languages and at the same time. It was a roar of prayer: a flow of words that seemed to ripple and dance across the large auditorium. I felt I was standing under a hot shower of faith. And I imagine this story in the same way.

Peter and John, on their return from custody, meet up with this fast-growing Christian community. Their instinct is corporate prayer before corporate strategy, and they lift their voices before God together. Before they mention their own urgent needs, they lose themselves in adoration of the God of all creation.

When they heard this, they raised their voices together in prayer to God. 'Sovereign Lord,' they said, 'you made the heavens and the earth and the sea, and everything in them.'

Acts 4:24

## RESPOND

Find a place where you feel comfortable to pray out loud. This may be familiar or new, but lift your voice to God and thank him that he is Lord of heaven and earth.

**Bible in a year:** 1 Kings 18,19; 1 Corinthians 16

# There we sat; there we wept

### PREPARE

Grief and loss are inescapable human experiences. Today, recall the losses you have known: people, places or companion animals; maybe the loss of opportunity or even freedom. Sit and weep before God.

### READ

**Psalm 137**

### EXPLORE

Lament is the soundtrack of grief, with an impressive playlist in the psalms. It is reckoned that 42 of the 150 psalms in the canon are in this genre. Almost a third of Israel's songbook consists of songs of loss. And for many of us, that sounds about right. When I add up all the tears, bereavements, losses, disappointments and regrets, a theme of lament is there in the background.

This psalm is one of the more memorable laments, in large measure because of the chart-topping version released by the German band Boney M in 1978: 'By the Rivers of Babylon' (v 1). Strange that a song mourning the devastation of ancient Jerusalem in the sixth century BC should top the charts in the 1970s. And it's the loss of a place that's the emotional centre of this psalm. Jerusalem, the city of David, the nation's greatest king. Jerusalem, the place of the Temple, God's dwelling place, where heaven and earth came together. Jerusalem, home to a dispersed people, now a ruin. Jerusalem, the psalmist's highest joy. All now destroyed.

By the rivers of Babylon we sat and wept when we remembered Zion.

**Psalm 137:1**

### RESPOND

Where are your dear places, where you feel at home and close to God? Think of the faces of those you love and give thanks: 'Lord of all, I give you praise, my lament of praise.'

**Bible in a year:** 1 Kings 20,21; Nahum 1–3

**Scripture Union**

# A legacy of hope

································

Could you leave a gift in your will and ensure
the good news of Jesus is shared with
generations to come?

TO FIND
OUT MORE, VISIT
SU.ORG.UK/LEGACY OR
CALL **01908 856120**

'...we will tell the next generation the praiseworthy deeds of the
Lord, his power, and the wonders he has done.' **Psalm 78:4**

# The rise of a kingdom

The emergence of a new leader for a nation, organisation or church brings mixed emotions: hope and optimism, yet concern and anxiety. What will they be like? What changes will they bring?

1 Samuel 1–12 is the story of the rise of Israel's first king. The nation was emerging from the volatile period of the Judges, a time when 'everyone did as they saw fit' (Judges 21:25). God's chosen people had lost their way and had fallen into wickedness and apostasy. Even the priests called to lead the worship of God were evil and corrupt.

Here we will read of a woman of faith whose childlessness mirrors the barrenness of Israel. We will discover how the child she eventually bears is used to call the nation back to God. The child, Samuel, looms large in these chapters, and serves as a bridge between Judges and Kings. When Israel demands a king 'as all the other nations have' (1 Samuel 8:5), it is Samuel who warns them to be careful what they wish for. Yet at God's command he eventually anoints Saul as king.

As we ponder these chapters, we will find not just history but lessons for today: challenges about holy living, the importance of leadership, and how God draws near in darkest times. Ultimately, we will be reminded of God's faithfulness and provision, and his promise of a king to come who would be far greater than Samuel or Israel could ever imagine.

## About the writer
## Glenda Trist

Glenda lives with her husband in Melbourne, Australia, near to their grown-up children. Her pastoral work in a city hospital, and providing professional pastoral supervision to ministry workers, keeps her faith grounded, stretched and blessed. She enjoys writing for *Daily Bread* because it provides opportunity for her to dig deep into God's Word, discovering more about him.

# Remember me

## PREPARE

**Reflect upon a time when you felt abandoned, worthless, hurt or bitter. What were your conversations with God like then?**

. . . . . . . . . . . . . . . . . . . . . . . . . . . . . . . . . . . . . . . . . . . . . . . . . . . . . . . . . . . . . . . .

## READ

**Samuel 1:1–28**

## EXPLORE

At the heart of Samuel's birth narrative, we meet Hannah. Hannah was barren, causing her deep shame, grief and disgrace (vs 5–7). Women gained their worth by birthing sons. The annual pilgrimage to worship God only magnified Hannah's grief. A festival of joy and feasting was for Hannah a time of weeping and fasting. How could she celebrate God's blessings when God had not blessed her with children? He was the source of her problem. Hannah had no appetite for celebrating in God's presence.

Weeping with bitterness of soul, Hannah reached desperation (v 7). Yet somehow she remembered her loving Lord; that ultimately, God was the One who would help her. Clinging to hope, she chose not to turn from God, but towards him (v 11). Note her passionate pleading (vs 10,12). Hannah's faith remembers who God is: loving, forgiving, active, faithful. And God graciously remembers Hannah (v 20).

Have you ever felt overwhelmed or struggling? For me, turning towards God has not always come easily. I am stubborn. But the homecoming with him is something freeing and beautiful. God yearns for us to turn towards him as Hannah does.

> She said, 'May your servant find favour in your eyes.' Then she went her way and ate something, and her face was no longer downcast.
>
> **1 Samuel 1:18**

## RESPOND

Turn towards God now. Is there something that needs dealing with that compromises your trust with God? What needs saying? What do you need to hear? Have that conversation with God now.

. . . . . . . . . . . . . . . . . . . . . . . . . . . . . . . . . . . . . . . . . . . . . . . . . . . . . . . . . . . . . . . .

**Bible in a year:** 1 Kings 22; Psalms 60,61

# Surprising reversals

## PREPARE

Remember the joy of prayers answered. Spend time praising our Lord for actively answering our prayers.

## READ

**1 Samuel 2:1–11**

## EXPLORE

Becoming a mother transformed Hannah's life: a child to love; shame turned to respect. Her response to God is a beautiful song of praise. Yet note that her child is not mentioned in the song. Hannah's focus was bigger than her son. God was her focus. That she could boast over those who once condemned her (v 1) was because of God himself. He was the Rock of Israel like none other (v 2). If God could turn the impossible into the possible in her life, then he could do the same if Israel would trust him.

Hannah's personal experience gives us a God-understanding to nourish even our lives. She encourages us to see a God of 'surprising reversals'. Barren becomes fruitful. Faithlessness becomes faithful. How many surprising reversals can you find in verses 4–8? Like Hannah, we are called to see God at work all around us, often in surprising ways. He has plans for his people if only we can trust him (vs 8b–10).

What encourages me in my hospital work is witnessing the gentle movement of God's miracles of transforming, healing, finding peace, prayers answered and celebrations. Hope is restored through God's loving presence among us. I am encouraged to note God's 'surprising reversals'.

'There is no one holy like the LORD; there is no one besides you; there is no Rock like our God.'

1 Samuel 2:2

## RESPOND

What currently keeps you strong with God? What reminds you that God is with you? Like Hannah, sing a song of praise out loud, right now.

**Bible in a year:** 2 Kings 1–3; Habakkuk 1–3

# Bad boys and linen

## PREPARE

**Where are you most vulnerable to temptation? Take time to sense the weight you carry from this. Share with God now. He awaits your turning towards him.**

## READ

**1 Samuel 2:12-26**

## EXPLORE

The writer is blunt. Eli's sons were wicked, deliberately and defiantly sinning against God.

The tabernacle contained the Holy of holies, where God dwelled among his people. Alarmingly, Eli's sons were priests-in-charge, polluting the tabernacle with intimidation and violence (vs 12–17).

Yet light and hope come. Glimpses of Samuel are given (vs 18–21,26) and the contrast between Samuel and Eli's sons is clear. Since a barren, faithful Hannah requested a child, God has been growing a faithful person after his own heart to love and lead his people – a youngster in a linen ephod (v 18). Such an apron signified a person called to serve in the Temple, the linen a sign of purity. Samuel grows in stature and favour before the Lord, God's gift, not just to Hannah but for Israel (v 26).

Today we need leaders like Samuel in the church and the community, not those like Eli's sons whose behaviour dishonours God. Let us be aware of the temptations that power can easily bring. Let us come to the One who can 'provide a way out so that you can endure it' (1 Corinthians 10:13).

> Eli's sons were scoundrels; they had no regard for the LORD.
>
> **1 Samuel 2:12**

## RESPOND

Ask God for guidance. Consider finding someone to whom you can be regularly accountable. Choose someone spiritually mature who you respect and feel safe with, a person who will gently challenge you when needed. Could you approach them this week?

**Bible in a year:** 2 Kings 4,5; Zephaniah 1–3

# So long, goodbye

## PREPARE
Pause a moment. Busyness calls, but push back on it. Unload, talking to God about how you are travelling. Remember he cares.

## READ
**1 Samuel 2:27–36**

## EXPLORE
Like me, do you find this passage hard to sit with? It is difficult hearing God, through his prophet, pour out frustration and sadness. Painful again to hear of Eli's sons' deliberate rejection and betrayal of God and Israel. His chosen priests have disgraced themselves and despised the One who had called them.

To be honest, there are days when I am discouraged and wearied by the really bad behaviour our world increasingly engages in, nation to nation, people to people. And discouraged by those who turn away from God, even in the church.

Where do we find the hope and nourishment? Unexpectedly there is much in this passage. Reread it slowly. God is broken-hearted. He too sits in a messy, broken world. He understands 'weary' and 'broken-hearted' more deeply than we ever could. We are not alone. We can take courage from his empathy. And there are the strong, precious promises that God makes to his people. He brings justice. He honours those who honour him (v 30). He raises up Samuel as a faithful priest and prophet who will speak God's word clearly to his people (v 35). Our sense of hopelessness fades away because of who God is.

'I will raise up for myself a faithful priest, who will do according to what is in my heart and mind.'

1 Samuel 2:35

## RESPOND
Choose a promise that stands out for you in today's passage. Contemplate how it nourishes your spirit. How might it affect your day? Praise God.

**Bible in a year:** 2 Kings 6,7; Haggai 1,2

# It's all happening

## PREPARE

Reflect on God's promises to reveal himself to you in his Word, a 'lamp for my feet' (Psalm 119:105). Look out for what God will reveal of himself.

## READ

**1 Samuel 3:1 – 4:1a**

## EXPLORE

The voice of God speaking to Samuel is such a loving, gentle story. Ears will tingle though. Something that will shock Israel is happening (v 11). And it's God's doing! Eli's corrupt family is on its way out! The young Samuel will be the new voice of God for Israel.

Under Eli there has been a famine of God's words and visions (v 1). Israel's loyalty to the Lord has waned. The old priest Eli is almost blind and unable to control his sons (vs 2,13). Through Samuel, he hears again of God's judgement (v 18). Now, it is to Samuel that God speaks. He has never before encountered God in such a personal way (v 7). God confirms his calling as a prophet, the one who will reveal God's ways to Israel (vs 19–21). God's presence is *with* him (v 19).

Like Israel, we need God's words in our life to ensure a personal relationship with God to keep us strong and faithful. We have Jesus as God's final revelation and the Bible as God's written Word. How wonderful that we are not alone. The Lord still speaks to us.

> The LORD continued to appear at Shiloh, and there he revealed himself to Samuel through his word. And Samuel's word came to all Israel.
>
> **1 Samuel 3:21 – 4:1**

## RESPOND

Staying grounded in God's Word helps us to know God and live a godly life in a complicated 'today'. How might you plunge deeper into God's Word – a Bible study group, conference or a Bible college subject, perhaps?

**Bible in a year:** 2 Kings 8,9; Psalms 62,63

# The heart or nothing

## PREPARE

**We live in a world that puts value on looking and sounding good. How does that align with God's call to the heart? Turn to God to seek his wisdom.**

## READ

**1 Samuel 4:1b–22**

## EXPLORE

'Why did the LORD bring defeat on us?' (v 3). This question follows Israel's shocking defeat by the Philistines. Concluding that God's absence is the problem, the people illicitly transport the Ark of the Lord's Covenant from Shiloh into the war camp (4:3b). Israel is trying to manipulate God to achieve their victory. It should be obvious that it's their unrighteousness, and that of Eli's sons, that is the real problem. The covenant promises of faithful obedience have been broken.

God continues to fulfil his words of judgement (2:30,34). In the next battle Israel loses their priests, Hophni and Phineas, and 30,000 soldiers (vs 10,11), and the Ark is captured (v 11). It is disastrous. The people get it wrong in thinking God is appeased by symbolic gestures. Israel needs to offer what God is truly looking for: faith like that of Hannah and Samuel.

The story concludes with Eli's daughter-in-law dying in labour (v 20). She calls her son Ichabod, meaning 'the glory of God has gone'. In a biblical cliffhanger, we are left with the question: Has God really abandoned his beloved Israel?

> The elders of Israel asked, 'Why did the LORD bring defeat on us today…?'
>
> **1 Samuel 4:3**

## RESPOND

What can we learn from our reading that Israel didn't? Pray that the Lord might help us seek consistency between our outer and inner lives. Ask his Spirit to renew our hearts and reflect his ways in us today.

**Bible in a year:** 2 Kings 10–12;  Zechariah 1,2

# High on love

## PREPARE

How beautiful are the sounds of praise, hearts stirred deeply experiencing God's unfailing love. Read Psalm 138 slowly... savouring the heart of God. Now reread it aloud, praising God.

## READ

**Psalm 138**

## EXPLORE

To praise 'with all my heart' in biblical times implied a well-spring of emotions, courage and all that was life-giving, erupting from deep inside. Today's psalm epitomises this. The psalmist's voice exuberantly sings his gratitude for God's help (vs 1–5). Note the psalmist's animated invitation for all nations to join in worshipping the Lord (vs 4,5). He is unapologetic and unabashed in his worship, lost in the wonder of the Lord. As you read, identify which phrases speak of your own experience of knowing God, even in times of trouble (v 7).

This psalm contrasts markedly with yesterday's reading. When Israel was defeated, there was no turning to God for help, nor moments of praise. It is difficult for praise to come easily to hearts which are deceitful and closed, hiding betrayal and apostasy. Perhaps you have noticed that when bitterness, cynicism or hurt enters your heart, you can feel like an observer in worship, rather than being able to participate in a heartfelt way. Let's choose to seek God's help to overcome this so that we can rediscover the spirit of overflowing, heart-felt worship that we find in this psalm: 'Your love, LORD, endures for ever' (v 8).

I will praise you, LORD, with all my heart ... I ... will praise your name for your unfailing love and your faithfulness.

**Psalm 138:1,2**

## RESPOND

What holds you back from worshipping? Challenge yourself today and dance (in private!) as you read this psalm. Use arms or feet to express your love to God.

**Bible in a year:** 2 Kings 13,14; Zechariah 3,4

# Samuel the rock!

## PREPARE

Pause and remember how you came to know the Lord Jesus. Who were the special people there to support you? Thank God for them.

## READ

**1 Samuel 6:21 – 7:17**

## EXPLORE

Across a wheat field finally appears the Ark of the Covenant. Excited but reluctant to offend God, nervous Israel sends the Ark to the backwater of Kiriath Jearim for safekeeping (6:20,21). Israel now knows that God's presence has returned! Amazingly the whole nation turns back to the Lord (v 2b). But how to approach God reverently? How to live as God's people? They have been living in moral anarchy and apostasy.

Samuel steps in. The boy who served God faithfully at the altar has become God's trusted spokesperson. Samuel teaches Israel to remember God and what his holiness requires (vs 3–6). He guides them to get rid of foreign gods and to repent sacrificially. At Israel's pleading, Samuel intercedes with God when Philistines return to attack (vs 8,9). God subdues them. Israel learns afresh that when they are faithful to God, he will answer them (v 12).

How blessed was Israel that Samuel was there to disciple and intercede for them. We all need 'Samuel's in our lives who will generously share God's wisdom with us and pray for us. We too are called to do the same for others (2 Timothy 2:2).

Samuel continued as Israel's leader all the days of his life.
**1 Samuel 7:15**

## RESPOND

God's special gift to Israel was Samuel. Is there a person who might need you to be a Samuel to them, who would value guidance and encouragement in the faith? Pray about it. Maybe share your thoughts with your pastor.

**Bible in a year:** 2 Kings 15,16;  Psalms 64,65

# Stubborn people

## PREPARE

'Do not conform to the pattern of this world, but be transformed by the renewing of your mind' (Romans 12:2). Reflectively consider what God might want from you.

## READ

**1 Samuel 8:1–22**

## EXPLORE

Israel wants a king! A king to rule instead of Samuel's corrupt sons. Mostly, however, a king to lead them into battle, so that they can be like other nations (vs 5,19,20). Ironically, God has already provided Israel's leaders when needed. He has led Israel to all her victories, sometimes without any battle. Israel rejects God as their great king; yet God still agrees to their request.

We read later that Israel's king of choice, Saul (9:2), will be a dismal failure. He recklessly disobeys God and Israel must bear the consequences. But God will not allow Israel to ruin his ultimate plan for his people. Their second king will be of God's choice (16:12,13).

We can be comforted in knowing that God honours our freedom to choose. But he also guides us through his Holy Spirit. He brings others who speak his wisdom into our lives. He greets repentance with acceptance and forgiveness. But, importantly, as with Israel, he will not let his purposes for our salvation be derailed because of our mistakes. Eventually the greatest King, the eternal Lord Jesus, will reign on earth when he comes again. God does not want us to be like other nations, but to be extraordinary (see Romans 12:2).

> 'When that day comes, you will cry out for relief from the king you have chosen, but the LORD will not answer you in that day.'
>
> **1 Samuel 8:18**

## RESPOND

What decisions are you facing? How could one decision become an extraordinary decision in God's eyes? Could you pray with someone else about this? Make a time to meet.

---

**Bible in a year:** 2 Kings 17,18; Zechariah 5,6

## Wednesday 5 June
### 1 Samuel 9:1–27

# We were expecting you!

## PREPARE

Have you experienced any 'God-coincidences' recently? What do these say to you? Thank God for these moments. Ask him to help you to notice them more often.

## READ:
**1 Samuel 9:1–27**

## EXPLORE

The large inner-city hospital where I work began with a handful of young Irish nuns wanting to share the love of Jesus with those in need. From a small cottage the hospital grew, based on the conviction that God would supply what was needed. They believed in a God of providence; a God who never 'sees' without acting in response to need; in God's faithful 'seeing to' the needs of the universe. A sense of divine providence remains today.

We see this God of providence here. The choreography is stunning. From the runaway donkeys (vs 3,4) to Saul receiving God's message on the way home (vs 9:27 – 10:1), everything works together to secure a king. Reread the passage, looking out for the 'coincidences'. Through this choreography, God ensures we know who really is in charge.

God heard Israel's request for a king. Yet Israel's kings are to be different. They will rule under God. God allows Saul to be king and guides him through his prophet Samuel. Later in their history, God will defeat Israel's enemies through their kings. This is God 'seeing to' Israel's needs. Recognising God's providence is an invitation: a call to be patient in adversity, thankful for provision and confident, for we see God at work.

> They went up to the town, and as they were entering it, there was Samuel, coming towards them on his way up to the high place.
>
> **1 Samuel 9:14**

## RESPOND
How might your prayers change if you believe that God acts on what he sees today? Ask for wisdom as you pray for others now.

**Bible in a year:** 2 Kings 19,20; Zechariah 7,8

# The making of a king

## PREPARE

What is your understanding of how the Holy Spirit works in your life? How are you conscious of his presence in your ministry?

## READ

**1 Samuel 10:1–27**

## EXPLORE

Have you ever felt God asking you to take on ministry in an area where you feel inadequate? For me, it usually revolves around upfront teaching. The old 'impostor syndrome' flares up, even to this day. But this is nothing compared to how Saul was probably feeling about being king of Israel.

Notice how the Lord cares for Saul, providing him with signs, affirmations and the guidance of Samuel. Saul's anointing is symbolic of his spiritual preparation for being king (v 1). God equips him to be a better king, through the empowerment of the Holy Spirit (v 6). Consider also how God cares for Israel by answering their request for a king to lead them in battle against their enemies. Note also how, as a 'theocratic' king, Saul has God with him.

If God cares like this for an unknown king and a nation who had rejected him,

how much more will he care for us when we step up in service for him. God will not desert us when we step out of our comfort zones and challenge ourselves for him. Instead, he promises to sustain and support us.

> 'The Spirit of the LORD will come powerfully upon you, and you will prophesy with them; and you will be changed into a different person.'
>
> **1 Samuel 10:6**

## RESPOND

Have you been asked to take on more in your ministry role? Are you feeling out of your comfort zone? Know that God is with you. Ask him for what you need.

**Bible in a year:** 2 Kings 21,22; Zechariah 9,10

1 Samuel 11:1–15

# How can this man save us?

## PREPARE

'Never be lacking in zeal, but keep your spiritual fervour, serving the Lord' (Romans 12:11). What does this mean for you?

. . . . . . . . . . . . . . . . . . . . . . . . . . . . . . . . . . . . . . . . . . . . . . . . . . . . . . . . .

## READ

**1 Samuel 11:1–15**

## EXPLORE

On returning home with his oxen, Saul is confronted with loud wailing and terrible news of his countrymen (v 2). Instantly brave and battle ready, he initiates a battle plan. Needing to rally and unite his people, he challenges them with his own dissected oxen. Messages are sent, a massive force of strength gathered and Israel comes 'out together as one' (v 7). The battle erupts upon the Ammonites before dawn and God's people are saved, united behind their king. Samuel invites all to celebrate their new king.

What makes Saul so different? Look again at verse 6. God's Spirit is present, instantly transforming him into the king Israel asked God for. Saul's Spirit-filled anger spurs him into battle. Recall Saul receiving the Holy Spirit at his anointing. 'You will be changed into a different person,' the prophet declared (1 Samuel 10:6). There is no other explanation!

Through Jesus we all have access to God's Spirit. Have you experienced becoming 'battle ready' through him? I spend significant time listening to folk. Listening deeply is hard work indeed. I need the Spirit's presence, providing discernment of what I really need to hear. It may be a quieter battle, but I am armed and strengthened for his work.

> When Saul heard their words, the Spirit of God came powerfully upon him, and he burned with anger.
>
> **1 Samuel 11:6**

## RESPOND

Ask God's Spirit to accompany you into each day. Watch and listen for what God would have you notice. Why not begin now?

. . . . . . . . . . . . . . . . . . . . . . . . . . . . . . . . . . . . . . . . . . . . . . . . . . . . . . . . .

**Bible in a year:** 2 Kings 23–25; Psalms 66,67

# Faithful service

## PREPARE

Stand quietly and imagine your life: all you can see before and behind. Where is God in all this? Where are you heading together?

## READ

**1 Samuel 12:1–25**

## EXPLORE

Have you ever sat with older people to hear their life stories? Older people often become quite reflective, trying to work out what the purpose of their life has been. They become thoughtful about what they want to pass on, especially to those they love.

This was Samuel. It is not surprising to know that what Samuel is most concerned about is the relationship between God and Israel. Since a youth he has lovingly served God and his people. Samuel has something to say that he wants them to hear. He takes the opportunity for a final farewell: a chance to share a legacy story. We hear of the Lord bringing the early Israelites out of Egypt, leading them with his constant presence through the wilderness, settling them into this Promised Land. God had delivered them from enemies, fought battles with them and provided leaders, including now a human king. Samuel calls on Israel to remember just how faithful God has been to them, so they will follow their God.

If you were to consider your own faith journey, in hindsight, what changes would you make? What change would you consider in your life now to better reflect your love of Jesus?

'But be sure to fear the LORD and serve him faithfully with all your heart; consider what great things he has done for you.'

**1 Samuel 12:24**

## RESPOND

Consider the faith legacy you want to pass on to your loved ones. What would you like them to know? How can you share this?

**Bible in a year:** 1 Chronicles 1–3; Zechariah 11,12

# The wonder of...

## PREPARE

What are the images or words of God that help you feel most comforted or reassured? Pray these right now, that you would know the reassurance of God's 'knowing you'.

. . . . . . . . . . . . . . . . . . . . . . . . . . . . . . . . . . . . . . . . . . . . . . . . . . . . . . . . . . . . . . . . . . . . . . .

## READ

**Psalm 139**

## EXPLORE

Late today, I was called to the bedside of a woman living her last hours. June shared her deep love for Jesus. But she was becoming anxious. We talked. We read June's favourite psalm together: Psalm 139.

Psalm 139 describes an experience of being one with God that is tender and beautiful. God knows us perfectly, far beyond what we know of ourselves (vs 1–6). There is nowhere where God is not; nowhere for us to hide, even in dark places (vs 7–12). God was there when we were made. When we awake, he is there still (vs 13–18). Because we love God, we hate all who stand against him (although now we remember Jesus' words in Matthew 5:43,44); our hearts need searching also, so we don't offend him (vs 19–24). What stands out for you in these words?

As we read together, June's face seemed to register the well-loved words, as if they had never been heard before. Slowly an almost tangible warmth moved across her face and being. She soaked up each word... each image... smiling that her Lord was so close and that she could never find somewhere where the Lord was not already awaiting her. Deep peace.

Before a word is on my tongue you, LORD, know it completely.

Psalm 139:4

## RESPOND

The wonder of God's love for us shines through this psalm. Blessed ourselves, let's celebrate by thanking God and deliberately sharing his love with another... perhaps someone lonely?

. . . . . . . . . . . . . . . . . . . . . . . . . . . . . . . . . . . . . . . . . . . . . . . . . . . . . . . . . . . . . . . . . . . . . . .

**Bible in a year:** 1 Chronicles 4–6;  Zechariah 13,14

Scripture Union

A BRAND NEW SCRIPTURE UNION HOLIDAY CLUB!

Grab your snorkel and plunge into the book of Matthew with *Deep Sea Divers*!

# Deep Sea Divers

Includes photocopiable resources and FREE EXTRAS online

A Scripture Union holiday club programme Great new ideas inspired by experience

Discover the depths of Jesus' love as you dive into his life, death and resurrection with children and young people.

FIND YOUR COPY AT: WWW.SU.ORG.UK/DEEPSEA
Also available at your local Christian bookshop

# Testimony to the truth

When I have some leisure time in London, I like to spend an afternoon in one of the big galleries. I have learned over the years that rather than rush through each room spending a few moments with each picture, I get a better experience by spending more time with just a few paintings. That way I can really see what is going on and what the artist is doing.

About the writer
**Toby Hole**

Toby is Director of Mission and Ministry in the Diocese of Sheffield, where he lives with his wife Amy, his three children and two tortoises. He previously worked in a church in London, and before ordination was a solicitor. When he isn't working, he can usually be found in a cinema or walking in the nearby Peak District.

Reading John's Gospel is a little like touring an art gallery. We can read through it quickly with each scene like a painting in a gallery. If we do that then we get a good idea of the story, but perhaps we miss John's finer details.

These finer details can be seen in the themes that run all the way through the Gospel, one of which is testimony: the testimony of other people about Jesus, and the testimony of Jesus about himself – especially his 'I am' sayings.

Chapters 5 to 7 centre on one of those 'I am' sayings – 'I am the bread of life' (6:35) – and they also look in detail at what it means to testify about Jesus. What authority does Jesus have to make these claims? How can these claims be trusted? These passages have sometimes been likened to a trial scene with lawyers arguing to and fro about who this man really is. As we read these passages, the same questions confront us. How might we answer them?

# Get up and pick up!

## PREPARE

Is there something on your heart that you have been asking of God for a long time? Bring it to him before reading this passage.

## READ

John 5:1–15

## EXPLORE

Thirty-eight years is a very long time to be ill (v 5). In a world without modern medicine, people will go to any lengths to find healing. The pool of Bethesda seemed to attract sick people seeking healing, in much the same way as some modern spa towns do.

We don't know why Jesus stopped beside this particular man. Perhaps he saw his despair. Perhaps, as with the man born blind later in the Gospel (ch 9), the healing of such a severe illness is intended to bring glory to God. His question, 'Do you want to get well?' sounds strange to us. We might answer, 'Obviously!' But Jesus does not enforce his healing on anyone. He respects this man's identity and integrity and is not here to show off his healing power. In fact, the healing is rather understated. Jesus simply tells the man to 'get up' and 'pick up your mat' before slipping away into the crowd. Jesus demonstrates that power lies in God and not in supposedly magic waters, but it is the person before him that is important, not point-scoring.

> When Jesus saw him lying there and learned that he had been in this condition for a long time, he asked him, 'Do you want to get well?'
>
> John 5:6

## RESPOND

Imagine that you are by the pool of Bethesda, and you see Jesus walking towards you. What will he ask you, and how will you answer? If your prayers are answered, will you tell others of Jesus' love?

**Bible in a year:** 1 Chronicles 7–10; Psalm 68

# Crossing over

## PREPARE

**Is there anything that you have thought, said or done that is bothering you? If so, tell Jesus that you are sorry, and know that you are forgiven.**

## READ

**John 5:16–30**

## EXPLORE

For some years I practised as a lawyer and so I have seen trials at first hand. Typically, there is a judge, a defendant and witnesses, and lawyers arguing for the defence and prosecution. You see similar elements in today's passage. The charge sheet against Jesus is Sabbath-breaking and blasphemy, two of the most serious offences in Jewish law. The prosecutors are out for a conviction.

Then the scene changes. Jesus is no longer the defendant but the judge. Because Jesus is the judge, the One who gives eternal life (vs 24–27), those who meet him are given a choice. They can believe his words and live eternally or turn from him and be condemned. Those prosecuting Jesus now find themselves placed in the dock!

For followers of Jesus this is good news. Sometimes we can feel like we are the defendants. We are aware of the things we have done wrong, and feel guilty.

We can sometimes feel that the world is condemning us, and we don't know how to respond. Jesus tells us that we need not fear because we have crossed over from death to life. We are forgiven and acquitted.

'Very truly I tell you, whoever hears my word and believes him who sent me has eternal life and will not be judged but has crossed over from death to life.'

**John 5:24**

## RESPOND

Do you feel forgiven in every area of your life, or are there still parts of your past that make you feel guilty? Imagine walking out of court with all charges dropped against you. You are free!

**Bible in a year:** 1 Chronicles 11–14; Malachi 1,2

# Mistaken identity

**PREPARE**

Ask God to show you something new about Jesus as you read today's passage. Be prepared for God to open your eyes to fresh insights about our Saviour.

**READ**

John 5:31–47

**EXPLORE**

We often think of the Jewish leaders in the New Testament as pantomime villains – after all, they are mostly responsible for Jesus' death. In fact, some Pharisees (like Nicodemus in chapter 3) become secret disciples and follow Jesus. The problem with the Pharisees isn't that they were faithless but that their faith blinded them to God's love.

I think that verses 39 and 40 are among the saddest in the New Testament: 'You study the Scriptures diligently … yet you refuse to come to me to have life.' The Pharisees spent their lives poring over God's word, trying to live according to the Law of Moses. They expected the Messiah to come, yet when Jesus stands before them, they don't recognise him.

The reason that Jesus doesn't fulfil their expectations is that in fulfilling God's great law of love he breaks the lesser law of the Sabbath (eg 5:9,10). It wasn't that Sabbath rest wasn't important, but God

doesn't take a day off from healing the world, and Jesus is continuing his Father's work. The Pharisees are passionately, and tragically, wrong. Can we sometimes get trapped by our own assumptions and miss what God might be saying to us?

'You study the Scriptures diligently because you think that in them you have eternal life. These are the very Scriptures that testify about me, yet you refuse to come to me to have life.'

John 5:39,40

**RESPOND**

Do we have ideas about God (perhaps given to us when we were young) that need challenging? How might we use scripture to give us a better picture of his love?

**Bible in a year:** 1 Chronicles 15,16; Malachi 3,4

## Thursday 13 June
### John 6:1–15

# Feasting with Jesus

## PREPARE
Think of something in your life, or perhaps in the news, that seems impossible to solve. Offer it in trust to Jesus.

## READ
**John 6:1–15**

## EXPLORE
As we read through chapter 6 of John's Gospel, we come across an important verse early on, which might be missed. Verse 4 says that the Jewish Passover festival was near. Passover, associated with the escape from Egypt, the wanderings in the desert and (for Christians) the Lord's Supper, fills almost every verse of the chapter, beginning with the feeding of the 5,000.

This miracle appears in all four Gospels, but John typically has his own slant. The five loaves and two fish are miraculously divided among thousands of people, and so great is the abundance that the disciples are sent to collect the leftovers. John alone records Jesus' words, 'Let nothing be wasted' (v 12). Jesus has fed the multitude but the food is not to be left to rot, nor are the crowd encouraged to take the food home for their own use. We don't know what the disciples did with the 12 basketfuls – perhaps

they were distributed among the poor and needy. God's generosity is so great that even thousands of hungry people cannot exhaust his provision.

It is unsurprising that the crowd want to make Jesus their king, but they don't realise that it is their spiritual as well as their physical hunger that Jesus has come to satisfy.

> When they had all had enough to eat, he said to his disciples, 'Gather the pieces that are left over. Let nothing be wasted.'
> John 6:12

## RESPOND
Are there areas of your life in which you can see God's generosity? How might you share God's gifts to you with others?

**Bible in a year:** 1 Chronicles 17,18; Galatians 1

# Treading the waves

## PREPARE

Read Psalm 29:3,4. Remind yourself of the power and majesty of God who created the universe and has revealed himself in Jesus Christ.

## READ

John 6:16–24

## EXPLORE

When they escaped Egypt, the Israelites crossed the Red Sea at night. Remembering the Passover reference earlier in this chapter (v 4), this helps us understand the disciples' surprising evening boat trip. To be caught in a storm in darkness far from shore must be truly terrifying, and the disciples are not reassured when they see a strange figure walking across the sea towards them.

At the Exodus God separated the sea so that the Israelites walked on dry land. Here, Jesus goes one step further (literally!). He walks upon the waves themselves. In Job 9:8 God is described as one who treads on the waves, and when Jesus says to his disciples, 'It is I; don't be afraid', he is using the 'I am' name for God (v 20). John is leaving us in no doubt who Jesus is claiming to be.

Once they realise it is Jesus, the disciples are willing to take him into the boat. He does not force himself upon them. Even in the middle of the storm they have a choice whether to accept Jesus or not. Is John saying something to us about how we should respond faithfully when facing our own storms?

> But he said to them, 'It is I; don't be afraid.'
> John 6:20

## RESPOND

Imagine that you are in a storm-tossed boat. Perhaps this reflects an aspect of your life at the moment. Jesus walks towards you. Will you invite him in?

**Bible in a year:** 1 Chronicles 19–21; Psalm 69

# Prove yourself!

## PREPARE

Imagine a loaf of freshly baked bread: the smell, the taste, the texture. As fresh bread satisfies so much of our human need, Jesus satisfies our spiritual need. What are you hungry for?

. . . . . . . . . . . . . . . . . . . . . . . . . . . . . . . . . . . . . . . . . . . . . . . . . . . . . . . .

## READ

**John 6:25–40**

## EXPLORE

I like to bake my own bread. But before baking, the dough needs to rest. This is called proving. Today's passage is also about bread and proving, but not quite in the same way.

Although Jesus has fed thousands from a pittance, the Jewish leaders remain suspicious of him. Prove yourself. Show us some evidence (v 30). Moses gave us manna from heaven: what can you do? They want to fit Jesus into their understanding of Israel's story. Is Jesus another prophet? Is he a second Moses? Do we also try to make Jesus fit into our own worldview?

Jesus won't allow himself to be put in a box. Instead, he declares that he is the fulfilment of Israel's history and hopes. 'I am the bread of life,' (v 48) he says – I am the One who brings you life. He has already shown how he can provide heavenly food, but that was simply a sign to show that he is the heavenly food. He is the One who nourishes us with eternal life (v 58). He is the One who will raise up all those who believe in him.

> Then Jesus declared, 'I am the bread of life. Whoever comes to me will never go hungry, and whoever believes in me will never be thirsty.'
>
> **John 6:35**

## RESPOND

If you had a friend who was hungry, you would give them food to eat. What will you give a friend who is spiritually hungry? How can you point them to the bread of life?

. . . . . . . . . . . . . . . . . . . . . . . . . . . . . . . . . . . . . . . . . . . . . . . . . . . . . . . .

**Bible in a year:** 1 Chronicles 22,23; Galatians 2

# Burning coals

## PREPARE

Think of an example of injustice in the news. How does it make you feel? How would you pray about it?

· · · · · · · · · · · · · · · · · · · · · · · · · · · · · · · · · · · · · · · · · · · · · · · · · · · · · · · · · · · · · · · · · · · · · ·

## READ

Psalm 140

## EXPLORE

Psalm 140 probably doesn't make it into many people's list of favourite psalms. It belongs to a category of cursing psalms and to read it can feel distinctly unchristian. After all, didn't Jesus clearly tell his followers to bless their enemies? What are we to make of praying that burning coals fall on those we do not like?

Many years ago, I did have cause to pray this psalm when I found myself working for a client who was so unpleasant and ungodly that I felt soiled even by being in his presence. 'Keep me safe, Lord, from the hands of the wicked; protect me from the violent' (v 4). Even if our contact with such people is thankfully rare, there are Christians in many parts of the world whose lives are threatened by living among the wicked and the violent. Would they pray Psalm 140 in a different way from us?

St Augustine believed that in the psalms Christ prays with and for his church. As we read them, we pray in his voice as much as ours. Read Psalm 140 with its cry for protection, justice and even vengeance as though it is the cry of Jesus for his people. And take encouragement from the faithful ending. The Lord does secure justice for the poor.

> Keep me safe, Lord, from the hands of the wicked; protect me from the violent, who devise ways to trip my feet.
>
> **Psalm 140:4**

## RESPOND

'Do not be overcome by evil, but overcome evil with good' (Romans 12:21). Are there ways in which you can overcome evil with good today?

· · · · · · · · · · · · · · · · · · · · · · · · · · · · · · · · · · · · · · · · · · · · · · · · · · · · · · · · · · · · · · · · · · · · · ·

**Bible in a year:** 1 Chronicles 24–27; Galatians 3

# You are what you eat

## PREPARE

Do we sometimes read Jesus' words without realising how challenging they are? As you read today's passage, put yourself in the minds of those hearing it for the first time. How do you react?

## READ

**John 6:41–59**

## EXPLORE

The Jewish leaders are understandably perplexed. How can Jesus be bread from heaven? They know his family tree. Who does he think he is? Jesus does not dial down his language. He becomes more extreme. Not only is he the bread of life, but those who eat his flesh and drink his blood will be raised up at the last day. Cannibalism, eating human flesh, is one of the most horrific of human acts, and to the Jews, Jesus' language was distasteful. For Christians, we might recall Jesus' words at the Last Supper (Luke 22:17–19). The bread that Jesus breaks is his body given for the sins of the world. John doesn't record the Last Supper in his Gospel, but could he be alluding to it here?

CS Lewis famously wrote that anyone who said what Jesus said was either insane, a criminal, or was telling the truth. Jesus won't allow his listeners to treat him as a wise rabbi from Nazareth whose parents are known and respected. Everyone who hears his voice is forced into a decision. Do we believe he is who he says he is (v 51)?

> 'Whoever eats my flesh and drinks my blood has eternal life, and I will raise them up at the last day.'
>
> John 6:54

## RESPOND

What does it mean for you to feed on Jesus? This may mean taking Holy Communion, or an inner disposition of faith and obedience. How might you be nourished by his life this week?

**Bible in a year:** 1 Chronicles 28,29;  Psalms 70,71

# Words of life

## PREPARE

Some Bibles have Jesus' words written in red letters as a way of highlighting them. Are there particular sayings of Jesus that you find particularly comforting or challenging?

## READ

John 6:60–71

## XPLORE

Jesus didn't go out of his way to win friends – he probably wouldn't have got far in the diplomatic service. His teaching in Capernaum proves too difficult for many of his listeners and John tells us that from that time many disciples turned back and no longer followed him (v 66).

Perhaps they had followed Jesus because they were impressed by the signs that he had performed, or they had enjoyed his sparring with the authorities. But now Jesus seems to have gone too far. Maybe they have picked up that following Jesus could lead them into trouble or danger. And yet, the words Jesus speaks are 'full of the Spirit and life' (v 63). Is that what also makes them difficult?

The twelve, for the time being at least, remain steadfast. Peter as usual is their spokesperson. They have followed Jesus from the beginning and believe that he is the Messiah, 'the Holy One of God' (vs 68,69). If they leave now, then who else will speak words of eternal life? Jesus, of course, knows that even the twelve are not as solid as they seem. He knows that one of them will betray him at the end. I detect some sadness in Jesus' words. Leadership can be lonely.

Simon Peter answered him, 'Lord, to whom shall we go? You have the words of eternal life.'

John 6:68

## RESPOND

Can you give encouragement to a Christian leader whom you know? What might you say or do to help them?

**Bible in a year:** 2 Chronicles 1,2; Galatians 4

# Knowing the time

## PREPARE

**Do you feel fully present to meet with God in scripture and prayer? Spend 60 seconds in silence before reading today's passage.**

· · · · · · · · · · · · · · · · · · · · · · · · · · · · · · · · · · · · · · · · · · · · · · · · · · · · · · · · · · · · · · · ·

## READ

**John 7:1–13**

## EXPLORE

In the modern world people use social media platforms such as Twitter and Instagram to project themselves and their opinions to a wider audience. In Jesus' time the best way to make a big splash was to be seen and heard at one of the big festivals in Jerusalem.

The Festival of Tabernacles was one of the biggest of the Jewish feasts, when the Jews remembered living in temporary shelters in the wilderness (Leviticus 23:33–43). Jesus' brothers advise him that if he is going to seize the moment and create a mass following, now would be the time to do it. After all, Galilee was a backwater. Jerusalem was where you needed to be if you wanted to make it big.

However, John makes it clear that Jesus' brothers don't have his best interests at heart (v 5). Jesus has a very different agenda from their worldly ambitions, and he is aware of the need to act within God's time rather than the world's. There will come a time when Jesus will openly make the journey into Jerusalem, but not yet (v 8). Jesus is not interested in public acclaim: he listens only to the voice of his Father. Can we hear God's voice above the noise of those around us?

Therefore Jesus told them, 'My time is not yet here; for you any time will do.'

John 7:6

## RESPOND

What might it mean for you to live and act in God's time rather than be pushed around by the world's priorities?

· · · · · · · · · · · · · · · · · · · · · · · · · · · · · · · · · · · · · · · · · · · · · · · · · · · · · · · · · · · · · · · ·

**Bible in a year:** 2 Chronicles 3–5; Galatians 5

# Whose glory?

**PREPARE**

The heavens declare the glory of God' (Psalm 19:1). How do you glorify God in your life?

. . . . . . . . . . . . . . . . . . . . . . . . . . . . . . . . . . . . . . . . . . . . . . . . . . . . . . . . . . . .

**READ**

John 7:14–24

**EXPLORE**

Two of the most impressive women of the past decade have been the campaigners Greta Thunberg and Malala Yousafzai. Through them the causes of the environment and women's rights have been greatly advanced. Both seem to care more about their areas of passion than their own reputations. The same cannot be said for everyone in public life.

Jesus is aware that some people accuse him of being an attention seeker while others praise him for his teaching. For many, it would be easy to let ego take over, but Jesus stresses that his teaching comes not from him but from God. It is important that he stresses this because some are suggesting that he is deceiving the people (v 12) and is a false prophet – a dangerous allegation. But false prophets act for their own glory, whereas everything Jesus does is for God's glory alone.

It is for this reason that the accusations against him for healing on the Sabbath are so wide of the mark (v 23). Jesus heals not to enhance his reputation but to demonstrate the glory of God in people made whole (v 18). We see God's glory shining through Jesus' every action. This is what makes him both popular with the people and a threat to the authorities. Their own motives are cast in a poor light.

'Whoever speaks on their own does so to gain personal glory, but he who seeks the glory of the one who sent him is a man of truth.'

John 7:18

**RESPOND**

Spend some time thanking God for the places and the people in which you see his glory shine.

. . . . . . . . . . . . . . . . . . . . . . . . . . . . . . . . . . . . . . . . . . . . . . . . . . . . . . . . . . . .

**Bible in a year:** 2 Chronicles 6,7; Galatians 6

# Water for the thirsty

## PREPARE

Read Psalm 63:1 a few times. Ask God to show you where you are thirsting for him and pray for his life-giving Spirit to refresh you.

## READ

**John 7:25–39**

## EXPLORE

Water played an important part in the Festival of Tabernacles (7:2). A procession of priests would go from the pool of Siloam to the Temple, where water would be poured out by the altar. This may have been part of a prayer for rain at the end of a dry season in Israel. Jesus often takes Jewish rituals and traditions and refocuses them on himself. We have already seen this in his bread of life teaching.

You can imagine how dramatic it would have been at this high point of the festival for Jesus to stand up and say that he is the one in whom true spiritual refreshment may be found. John, with hindsight, tells us that Jesus is referring to the gift of the Spirit who will be poured out on the disciples at Pentecost. Jesus may also be reminding his listeners of one of the great prophecies of Ezekiel where a mighty river of life flows out of the Temple making all things new (ch 47).

John also prepares us for that moment when Jesus gives up his spirit and blood and water flow from his side (vs 37–39). The life-giving and thirst-quenching gift of the Spirit comes when Jesus is glorified through his death on the cross.

'Whoever believes in me, as Scripture has said, rivers of living water will flow from within them.'

John 7:38

## RESPOND

Praise God for the great gift of his Son, through whom we have been given the gift of eternal life.

**Bible in a year:** 2 Chronicles 8,9; Psalm 72

# Not from Galilee?

## PREPARE

'Teach me your way, LORD, that I may rely on your faithfulness; give me an undivided heart, that I may fear your name' (Psalm 86:11).

## READ

John 7:40–52

## EXPLORE

Unlike Matthew and Luke, John doesn't tell us about Jesus' birth, so this is the only time in his Gospel that Bethlehem is mentioned. It is an intriguing bit of dramatic irony where the Pharisees are saying that Jesus can't possibly be the Messiah because the prophets say that the Messiah must come from Bethlehem. John is expecting his readers to be shouting, 'But Jesus *is* from Bethlehem!'

The Pharisees think that they know everything about Jesus. They know his parents and family; they know the region of Israel in which he has been brought up; and none of this measures up to their idea of what the Messiah should look like. Their prejudice against Jesus' background has blinded them to the miracles that he has performed and his accomplished preaching which dazzles the crowds. Coming from Jerusalem, we might even call them the metropolitan elite. They have contempt for the crowd who are uneducated, and dissenting voices like Nicodemus are quickly shouted down (v 52).

At the beginning of his Gospel, John tells us that Jesus came to his own but his own did not receive him (John 1:11). Perhaps Jesus' background was simply too ordinary for them to see God at work.

> 'Does not Scripture say that the Messiah will come from David's descendants and from Bethlehem, the town where David lived?'
>
> John 7:42

## RESPOND

In our desire to see God do spectacular things, do we sometimes miss what he is doing in the ordinary? Pray for fresh eyes to see God at work.

**Bible in a year:** 2 Chronicles 10–12;  Ephesians 1

# Perfumed prayers

### PREPARE
**Engage one of your senses as you pray today. Perhaps you may like to listen to music, look at a picture or hold something in your hand.**

### READ
**Psalm 141**

### EXPLORE
This psalm describes an experience common to us all. David is surrounded by ungodly men who are inviting him to join them in evil, and David is struggling with temptation. We know from the Old Testament histories that David did not always find temptation easy to resist. He prays that God will protect his mouth and his heart, and even that a righteous man might strike him in order to teach him wisdom. David seems torn between the 'delicacies' that the wicked offer him (v 4) and their ultimate destruction, vividly described in verses 6 and 7.

The beauty of the psalm lies particularly in the first two verses. David pictures the evening sacrifice when the priest would burn costly incense, making holy the offering. As the smoke ascended and the smell pervaded the sanctuary, so worshippers would imagine their prayers rising towards God. David is imaginatively joining his prayers to the sacrifice, asking God to hear him and save him.

We might protest that David is putting the responsibility for making the right choice in God's hands, rather than his own, but Jesus also taught us to pray, 'lead us not into temptation' (see v 4). This psalm is a good one to pray when we doubt that our resolution will hold.

> May my prayer be set before you like incense; may the lifting up of my hands be like the evening sacrifice.
>
> **Psalm 141:2**

### RESPOND
Pray the Lord's Prayer, focusing particularly on any area of temptation that you would like to be delivered from.

**Bible in a year:** 2 Chronicles 13–15; Ephesians 2

# A roller-coaster message

## About the writer
**Esther Bailey**

Esther lives with her husband John in north-east England, close to the Angel of the North. She is working with URC churches in Gateshead, Chester-le-Street and Stanley to engage with children and families not previously part of the church. Esther and John love exploring new areas in their aged campervan.

Isaiah lived and prophesied about 700 years before Jesus was born. He prophesied during the reigns of kings Uzziah, Jotham, Ahaz and Hezekiah, being a contemporary of Hosea and Micah. (Elijah, Elisha, probably Obadiah, also Joel, Jonah and Amos had already come and gone; Jeremiah, Daniel and Ezekiel were yet to come.) This period of Judah's history is told in 2 Kings 15–21 and 2 Chronicles 26–33.

On the world stage at this time, there are several superpowers vying for world domination – the Egyptians, the Assyrians and the Babylonians are all competing for supremacy, and Israel and Judah are little countries caught in the middle. However, size and strength were not really the issues – what mattered was who or what they trusted and venerated. The history of Israel is a long list of kings who 'did evil in the sight of the Lord' and so, in 722 BC, God allowed the Assyrians to destroy Israel and carry the people off into captivity.

By contrast, three of the four Judean kings mentioned above did 'what was right in the eyes of the LORD' (eg 2 Chronicles 26:4) although two came with the caveat that they allowed the people to continue to offer sacrifices and burn incense to idols and false gods.

Into this situation, Isaiah proclaimed his message, which is a roller coaster of judgement and hope – God is going to punish the nation for their rejection of him, but he is also going to restore them and bring about restored relationships and peace (1:26,27).

# A broken-hearted parent

## PREPARE

'It's amazing when someone can break your heart, but you still love them with all the little pieces' (Anon). Thank God for his enduring love for you.

## READ

**Isaiah 1:1–20**

## EXPLORE

Imagine you have a child into whom you have invested untold time, effort, financial resources, emotion – everything you could; but they choose to reject you and all the values you tried to instil in them. You feel angry, hurt and broken-hearted. However, as you watch them damage themselves with the choices they continue to make, you are also filled with compassion and long to draw them back to you and protect them. (Maybe you don't have to imagine – maybe this is your experience. Take comfort from the fact that God knows and understands.)

This is how God describes his relationship with his people, a broken-hearted parent pleading with his rebellious children. Read through the passage again, picking out phrases that describe God's anger, his hurt, his compassion and his longing for restoration. What over-riding emotion stands out for you? I was surprised to see how much it hurt God to see his people hurting themselves in their rebellion (eg v 5), and how reluctant he seems to mete out punishment (eg v 20).

> 'I reared children and brought them up, but they have rebelled against me.'
>
> **Isaiah 1:2**

## RESPOND

Reflect on your relationship with Father God. When have you been the eager child, keen to stay close and obedient? Or when have you taken his love for granted, been disobedient and wayward? Listen to what God has to say about his relationship with you.

**Bible in a year:** 2 Chronicles 16,17; Psalm 73

# Undiluted righteousness

**PREPARE**

'The righteousness of the blameless makes their paths straight' (Proverbs 11:5). Search Proverbs (for example, using Bible Gateway) to discover more about God's attitude to righteousness. What value is there in pursuing a life of righteousness?

**READ**

Isaiah 1:21–31

**XPLORE**

I wonder if the people were a bit surprised to hear Isaiah pronounce God's judgement on them. After all, they had a reputation for justice and righteousness (v 21), they were offering frequent sacrifices (v 11), they were vocal pray-ers (v 15) and their kings did what was right (2 Kings 15:3,34; 18:3). What more could God want?! And yet there were problems (eg v 7), and their worship practices had become meaningless rituals (vs 10–15).

The problem was that they diluted their righteousness with unrighteousness. They worshipped idols (v 29), they did not support the vulnerable in their society (v 23) and the leaders were dishonest (v 23). Just as a bit of dirt on a clean T-shirt makes the T-shirt dirty, so a bit of unrighteousness in a righteous society makes the society unrighteous.

But this passage also contains words of hope along with the judgement. God describes himself as a goldsmith, getting rid of the impurities in the precious metal, and making it pure again (vs 25–27).

> 'I will thoroughly purge away your dross and remove all your impurities.'
>
> Isaiah 1:25

**RESPOND**

'God made him who had no sin to be sin for us, so that in him we might become the righteousness of God' (2 Corinthians 5:21). God sets a high value on undiluted righteousness. Thank him for the price he paid to make you righteous.

# A picture of perfect peace

## PREPARE

In a world of increasing stress, anxiety and interpersonal or international conflict, how do you picture peace? What images come to mind?

## READ

**Isaiah 2:1–5**

## EXPLORE

Most of our readings this week are a mixture of judgement and hope – today's is solely a message of hope, which is repeated almost word for word in Micah 4:1–3. Did the Holy Spirit give the same message to both Isaiah and Micah who were contemporaries? Did one of them copy the other, or perhaps they were both quoting another anonymous prophet? We don't know, but the repetition challenges us to take note!

A stereotypical beauty pageant contestant might have claimed that what society needs is 'world peace' but without offering any idea what that looks like and how it could be achieved. Here, Isaiah describes the Messiah's rule as bringing about 'world peace'. It will be a time when worshipping God will be a central focus throughout the world (v 2). All people will acknowledge God as Lord and will want to follow his ways (v 3).

There will still be disagreements and conflicts, but they will be settled fairly and decisively (v 4). Money currently spent on defence and weapons of war can be redirected into food production and ensuring the well-being of all (v 4). We look forward to that time!

> Come, descendants of Jacob, let us walk in the light of the LORD.
>
> Isaiah 2:5

## RESPOND

After painting the picture of God's future reign on earth, Isaiah challenges his readers to be counter-cultural and to choose to live under God's reign now (v 5). What does it mean to you to 'walk in the light of the Lord' today?

**Bible in a year:** 2 Chronicles 21–23; Ephesians 4

# Whom do you trust?

## PREPARE

Idols are things we put our trust in. They are not God, but we treat them like they are. We hold them with a sacred reverence that should only be given to God.'* Do you have any idols?

. . . . . . . . . . . . . . . . . . . . . . . . . . . . . . . . . . . . . . . . . . . . . . . . . . . . . . . . . . . . . . . . . . . . . . . . . .

## READ

Isaiah 2:6–22

## EXPLORE

Reading about idol worship in the Old Testament, I wonder how people could drift so far away from God that they worship a bit of wood or stone. And yet, how tempting is it to give in to superstition or other ungodly practices that we see around us (v 6)? Money and accumulation of material things (v 7) can become idols. Nations trust in military strength (v 7) rather than looking to God. And people rate themselves according to their own abilities and achievements (v 8).

An idol is anything or anyone who takes the place of God in our lives. We may not physically put offerings on an altar, but how many children are sacrificed for the sake of a career, or a new relationship?

What idols do you see in your society? What about your own life? Many of these things are not wrong necessarily;

the danger is when they become more important to us than God – and we are all at risk!

> Their land is full of idols; they bow down to the work of their hands, to what their fingers have made.

Isaiah 2:8

## RESPOND

In 1 Chronicles 29:14 David prays, 'Everything comes from you, and we have given you only what comes from your hand.' Ask God to help you keep this perspective on the people and things in your life.

S Claiborne and M Martin, *Beating Guns: Hope for People Who are Weary of Violence*, Brazos Press, 2019

. . . . . . . . . . . . . . . . . . . . . . . . . . . . . . . . . . . . . . . . . . . . . . . . . . . . . . . . . . . . . . . . . . . . . . . . . .

**Bible in a year:** 2 Chronicles 24,25; Ephesians 5

# Indictment and judgement

## PREPARE

'... And what does the LORD require of you? To act justly and to love mercy and to walk humbly with your God' (Micah 6:8). Reflect on this verse.

## READ

**Isaiah 3:8 – 4:1**

## EXPLORE

In these verses, Isaiah pictures a court room, with God as judge. God's people have sinned in what they have said and what they have done (v 8). Even their facial expressions (v 9) and their posture (v 16) reveal their arrogance and selfishness. They not only have disregard for the poor; they have robbed them to enrich themselves (vs 14,15).

God's judgement is to replace all their finery with humiliation, defeat and captivity (3:17 – 4:1). Notice the contrast in verse 24 as Isaiah repeats 'instead of ...' (Annie Vallotton's illustration in the Good News Bible shows this graphically.)

Two categories of people are singled out for God's judgement: the leaders and the women. Women are particularly castigated, perhaps because of the impact mothers have on their children. If they are living for false values, what hope is there for the next generation?

While God pronounces judgement on the wicked, he promises blessing and protection to the righteous (v 10). However, Daniel, Nehemiah, Mordecai (from Esther's story) and many other God-followers were taken into captivity with all the rest. How did God keep his promise to them?

> The LORD takes his place in court; he rises to judge the people.
>
> Isaiah 3:13

## RESPOND

Listen to or read the lyrics of Tim Hughes' song 'God of Justice' (www.worshiptogether.com/songs/god-of-justice/). Turn the words into a prayer for yourself, your church and your society.

**Bible in a year:** 2 Chronicles 26–28; Psalm 74

# Future fruitfulness

## PREPARE

Reflect on the past few years. When have you been particularly aware of God's presence with you, or experienced his care and protection? How has his fruit been evident in your life? Praise him for his faithfulness to you.

## READ

### Isaiah 4:2-6

## EXPLORE

After judgement comes hope. After punishment, a time of restoration and then fruitfulness. The 'Branch of the LORD', mentioned several times in the Old Testament, is a reference to the Messiah. Through the redeeming work of the Messiah, God's people will be made holy and washed clean (vs 3,4). In particular, the women who were castigated in chapter 3 will be cleansed by the Lord himself. God doesn't just judge; he also restores and uplifts.

God's presence will be as real and obvious as it was for the Israelites in the wilderness who followed a pillar of cloud by day and a pillar of fire by night (v 5). In this future time, there may still be overpowering heat, and storms and rain, but God's presence will be a canopy providing shelter, protection and safety (v 6). Whatever life throws at us, God is our refuge and strength!

How wonderful is God's work in restoring his people! The words 'glory' or 'glorious' are used three times in just five verses.

'In that day the Branch of the LORD will be beautiful and glorious, and the fruit of the land will be the pride and glory of the survivors in Israel.'
**Isaiah 4:2**

## RESPOND

'I am the vine; you are the branches … I chose you … so that you might go and bear fruit' (John 15:5,16). Pray that God's fruitfulness will be shown through you so that his glory will be seen in your community.

**Bible in a year:** 2 Chronicles 29,30; Ephesians 6

# Choosing to trust

## PREPARE

**'You are my hiding place / you always fill my heart with songs of deliverance. / Whenever I am afraid I will trust in you.'\***

## READ

**Psalm 142**

## EXPLORE

In the time of Isaiah, the Israelites were trusting in all sorts of things – wealth, alliances with other countries, their forms of religion – but they weren't trusting in God. In this psalm, David is feeling trapped, tricked, deserted by friends and supporters, weak and unable to help himself – but he knows whom he can trust. As he states his desperation in this psalm, each alternate verse (vs 1,3,5,7) sees him turning back to reliance on God, deliberately choosing to look beyond the immediate difficulties and to see things in relation to God's strength and care.

This is not to minimise the difficulties David was facing – physically his life was in danger, his reputation was in tatters, his relationships broken and absolutely everything was a mess (see 1 Samuel 24:1–3). But he knows that God is aware of all that is happening to him (v 3), that God is a refuge (v 5), that God

is David's inheritance, not just after he dies, but now, 'in the land of the living'. David knows God is good, and so he appeals to God to save him, so that he can tell others of the goodness of God.

> When my spirit grows faint within me, it is you who watch over my way.
>
> **Psalm 142:3**

## RESPOND

**Use this psalm as a template for your own prayer. Begin with a direct appeal to God, tell him something you are concerned about and remind yourself what God is like. Finish with a pledge about your relationship with God.**

\*Michael Ledner, 'Hiding Place', https://hymnary.org/tune/hiding_place_ledner

**Bible in a year:** 2 Chronicles 31,32;  Luke 1:1–38